THE BLACK ECONOMY IN ENGLAND
SINCE 1914

EDWARD SMITHIES

The Black Economy in England since 1914

GILL AND MACMILLAN
HUMANITIES PRESS

Published in Ireland by
Gill and Macmillan Ltd
Goldenbridge
Dublin 8
with associated companies in
Aukland, Dallas, Delhi, Hong Kong,
Johannesburg, Lagos, London, Manzini,
Melbourne, Nairobi, New York, Singapore,
Tokyo, Washington
© Edward Smithies 1984
0 7171 1142 3

Published in 1984 in USA and Canada by Humanities Press Inc.
Atlantic Highlands, New Jersey 07716

Library of Congress Cataloging in Publication Data

Smithies, Edward.
    The black economy in England since 1914.

    Includes bibliographical references.
    1. Black market — Great Britain — History — 20th century.
    2. Employee theft — Great Britain — History — 20th century.
    3. Tax evasion — Great Britain — History — 20th century.
    4. Informal sector (Economics) — Great Britain — History —
    20th century. I. Title.
    HF5482.65.G7S64 1984 364.1'33 84-6516
    ISBN 0-391-03114-7

Print origination in Ireland by
Print Prep Ltd, Dublin
Printed in Hong Kong

Contents

Contents

NOTE

The United Kingdom adopted a system of decimal currency in 1971; Since most of this book is set before decimalisation, money values are expressed in the old system of pounds, shillings and pence (£ s d). There were twelve pence in each shilling, and twenty shillings in each pound.

1
Introduction

In recent years references in the press to the black economy have become common. Sometimes they give an account of the activities of the people involved; sometimes an attempt is made to calculate its size or rate of growth. On 22 July 1981 the *New Standard* carried a front page headline, 'The £4000m Swindlers'. This began a report about the impact on tax revenues of tax fiddlers, moonlighters and casual workers. The Public Accounts Committee of the House of Commons had estimated that evasion accounted for the loss of as much as 20 per cent of the entire yield of income tax. The Committee found particularly disturbing the possibility that evasion was becoming 'socially acceptable' and would spread to other areas of the economy. It drew attention to casual and agency workers who turned themselves into one-man companies to avoid tax, and to the newspaper, hotel and licensed trades. There, managements knowingly employed the same people even though they used false names and addresses each time they were paid. The Inland Revenue responded to the report by announcing that investigative procedures would be stepped up, PAYE records more thoroughly inspected and special offices to deal with tax evasion strengthened and extended.

In the same month, on 6 July 1981, *The Guardian* reported that a growing problem of the recession was caused by businessmen who were 'turning to fraud to save their companies or to salvage something from the crashed firms'. Some were trying to cope with the impact of the economic crisis on their legitimate companies by going 'the one step beyond bad business practice to criminality' to keep them afloat. 'The young inheritors of established family businesses do not want to face the shame of closing the firm their grandfathers and fathers built up.' Others decided that the collapse of the business was inevitable and were trying to seize some of the assets before it was too late. The police were alarmed by these developments, yet 'a large metropolitan county' had as few as twenty-five police officers enquiring into 'the biggest surge in white collar crime since the collapse of the property market in 1973-4'. The Metropolitan Police estimated that the sum at risk in their investigations was always around nine figures. Fraud was big business.

Meanwhile reports of the results of investigations into aspects of the black economy appear frequently. In March 1983 five men were jailed after vast frauds had been uncovered at Devonport dockyard. Two directors and the secretary of a building firm had conspired with a Department of Environment surveyor to cheat the dockyard authorities over the price of building work.[1] In November 1979 an inquiry was opened into petty pilfering which 'grew into one of the biggest investigations ever launched by Ministry of Defence police'.[2] A few weeks later the National Health Service estimated that recorded cases of theft, fraud and arson in hospitals cost them £774,340 in 1980-81. They claimed that 'large-scale pilfering of nappies, food, drugs, household goods, and cash' was going on every day in their hospitals.[3] Pilfering is also a problem in industry. A shop steward at British Leyland's Longbridge plant organised a network of pilferers who stole car parts. He told police 'when I collect the dues from the lads I have the freedom of the East Works and I just put a few things in my pockets.' The police set a value of £37,000 on the articles they were able to recover.[4] London Transport predicted that in 1983 it would lose £7.5 million as a result of frauds by its staff − 1 per cent of its income.[5] It sometimes seems, to quote a headline in the *Sunday Mirror*, that all 'Britain [is] on the Fiddle'.[6] 'There are fiddlers among the honest in every job . . . One hundred million pounds worth of goods "fall off lorries" and disappear every year. The British Road Haulage Association put it another way. They say the goods are carefully "lifted" from the lorries − or were never put aboard in the first place . . . In every big office and factory there is someone flogging cutprice watches, radios,

jewellery. Everyone knows that they are stolen goods . . .'
The Sun observed much the same phenomenon: 'Britain is a
nation of fiddlers . . . 2 per cent of everything made and sold
in Britain is pinched . . . Everyone is at it . . . from the shop-
floor to the board room.'[7]

It would be possible to go on adding similar cases and comments almost without limit: the difficulty is to know whether
the cases are typical, what their significance is in terms of the
whole economy, and whether the number and value of them
is growing. Unfortunately, no two authorities on the subject
are able to agree on an answer.

In 1977 Sir William Pile, then chairman of the Board of
Inland Revenue, estimated that the black economy accounted
for approximately 7½ per cent of gross national product.
His successor, Sir Lawrence Airey, agreed four years later
that the Inland Revenue still worked on the basis of that
figure even though it was not supported by systematic evidence. This implied that some £4 billion annually of potential tax revenue was lost by the Exchequer, an amount
that might have solved the British government's financial difficulties if it had been recovered. Airey believed that the
black economy was not expanding in real terms.[8]

The Institute of Fiscal Studies disputed these figures and
argued that the size of the black economy was about 2 per
cent to 2½ per cent of GNP. They derived their estimate
from the Family Expenditure Survey, basing their calcula-
tions on the gap between the incomes and expenditures of
individuals and households. They assumed that households
which spent markedly more than their declared income had
been participating in the black economy.[9] These findings
were dismissed by Sir Lawrence Airey who pointed out that
only 70 per cent of those asked by FES to give information
in fact did so.[10] He suggested that the other 30 per cent
might well know more about what was happening in the black
economy.

Professor Feige of Wisconsin University also attacked the
estimate worked out by the IFS. He argued that self-employed
people (who are generally thought to include a high proportion of tax dodgers) had tended not to reply to the FES. He
estimated that the black economy might account for as much

as 15 per cent of the country's income, or £9 billion a year, a figure he based on the amount of money people used for day-to-day buying and selling.[11]

The main obstacle in the way of a convincing estimate was the lack of systematic information. As Adrian Smith pointed out: 'A strong temptation emerges to draw firm and strong, and possibly heroic, conclusions . . . but a certain degree of academic integrity should prevail. It cannot be emphasised too strongly that this is a field in which it is more than usually difficult to obtain information, which is, by definition or desire, hidden, submerged or camouflaged in some form or other.'[12] The danger of projecting national estimates from limited evidence may be illustrated by examining the claim that workers 'fiddled' £705 million a year from their customers, a figure much quoted in press reports in the late 1970s. This figure originated with the Outer Circle Policy Unit's inquiry into the 'hidden economy' (which it describes as 'all those forms of personal reward which do not appear in official audits, whether they are employers' audits or official income statistics'.[13]) The 'fiddling' figure was in fact arrived at by 'projecting' the results of a single study of what happened in a bakery.[14] Until more comprehensive evidence is provided it is wise to approach statistical projections of the size of the black economy with caution. A range of estimates from 2 per cent to 15 per cent is so large as to be almost meaningless while a recent international comparison describes the 'informal' economy as amounting to between 1 per cent and 40 per cent of a nation's GDP.[15]

If such difficulties arise in estimating the size of the black economy today, the problem will be correspondingly greater for earlier periods. Yet a measure is needed to balance the anecdotal and impressionistic evidence which, though interesting and revealing, in itself cannot be used as a foundation for generalisations about the size and significance of the black economy. On the question of whether it is growing or changing, a historical perspective would shed useful light. It is proposed therefore to study the history of the black economy in certain areas of England from the period of the First World War to the late 1960s. The term 'black economy' will be understood as comprising those economic activities which were illegal and which those in authority (the ministries, employers and police) were anxious to suppress. This study will therefore examine principally the history of black markets, tax fraud, smuggling and pilfering.

There are, however, limitations to a work of this kind. No statistical series exists giving details of black economy offences. The First World War saw the publication of *The National Food Journal* which attempted a national survey of black market prosecutions but nothing similar was tried in the Second World War or in any period of peacetime. It is necessary therefore to rely on reports of court cases to find out what has been happening. To make this task manageable for a period of over fifty years it is proposed to concentrate on a limited number of towns. These have been chosen for their diversity, not because they are 'typical'. In studying the black economy, it is not possible to extrapolate a national picture from typical local experience. Black economies are as different from one another as 'legitimate' local economies. Their policing is also subject to policy changes. An historian of crime in the nineteenth century has written: 'We shall never be really clear how much of the recorded increase ... reflected a "real" increase, and how much was the product merely of administrative and attitudinal change.'[16] By concentrating on a limited number of towns it will be possible to explore these changes more thoroughly. As David Philips has pointed out, 'the national average lumps together agricultural and industrial, rural and urban, rich and poor areas. ... If one wants to see how patterns of criminal activity and law enforcement might relate to the pattern of employment in an area, to its social, economic and industrial structure, ... it is necessary to go beneath the surface of the national statistics, and concentrate on one town or area.'[17]

Many black economy offences are by their nature hidden. Even when they are discovered they do not always come to the attention of the courts. In 1962 J.P. Martin published an important study of pilfering. He found that 'all' firms were careful to avoid calling in the police when they discovered that their employees had stolen from customers. Even when the company itself was the loser the larger firms called in the police in only 31 per cent of cases while the smaller ones did so in only 21 per cent.[18] With many black market offences the decision whether to prosecute was taken at meetings of food control committees and was often the result of a vote. In other cases the decision rested with the police or the Director of Public Prosecutions. They would not start proceedings unless they felt the evidence was strong enough to provide a good chance of securing a conviction. It follows that figures of court convictions for black economy crimes are not a measure of all the black economy activities that took place. Minor instances might never be reported or could be overlooked. The evidence in more serious ones might be considered insufficient for a prosecution to be initiated. But if those involved repeatedly broke the law and thereby posed a real threat to the management of the economy in wartime or to the profits of the firm for which they worked it seems improbable that the authorities would not sooner or later secure a verdict in court against them. Therefore a comparison of serious[19] offences will show the black economy in its most threatening aspect. The result will not be a definite statement about the precise size of the black economy: in the nature of the evidence it seems unlikely that that will ever be possible. But it will show for the towns in this study whether the number of serious offences altered significantly over time, whether those involved were able to create 'a market' and whether the authorities were ever in danger of losing control of the situation.

As long as the black economy does not pose a threat to management of the economy it is susceptible to government control of its extent. The DPP can decide to prosecute or not in a case of tax fraud, a local food control committee may vote to overlook an instance of black marketeering *this time*, an employer decide to prosecute pilfering employees where last year he warned them. Such decisions are made according to the perceptions of those in control and may vary as much because of the general economic situation or the profit and loss account as they are a response to a rise in the number of black market crimes or a surge in the number of thefts at work. These numerous separate decisions may determine whether the black economy looks 'smaller' or 'larger' one year than another. At the same time the authorities are able to monitor what is happening for early signs of more serious developments. It will be seen that in the towns in this study these did not materialise. The authorities remained in control throughout. Even in periods of severe economic strain — such as the Second World War and its aftermath — the number of prosecutions for serious offences remained small. In the few cases in which the black economy had seemed to be taking on more ominous dimensions the perpetrators were sooner or later hit hard, either by imprisonment or heavy fines. However, two qualifications must be made to these statements. They apply to the towns studied here. A survey of what happened in a different group of towns might produce a different picture. Secondly, they are true of the period between 1914 and 1968. In the years since 1968, the situation may have been changing.

In selecting five towns for this book I have sought to include as wide a variety of economic and social histories as is possible within the limits of the study. I wished to compare a seaport with shipbuilding as well as dockyards and a substantial import-export trade; a northern industrial town dominated by a nineteenth-century staple industry, with a largely working-class population; a midlands industrial centre with a diverse economy that included expanding and declining sectors; a retail and leisure centre with a growing industrial base, which had also a significant proportion of its population in white-collar occupations; and an area of one of the great cities with a range of occupations and industries gathered in a variety of workplaces including large and small factories, workshops and sweatshops. Ideally one or more of these towns would serve as a market centre for the surrounding agricultural area, and another would have a reputation for criminal activity. Several British towns fit easily into each of these categories: those chosen for study here (Birkenhead, Barnsley, Walsall, Brighton and Hove, and the districts of north and east London 'covered' by Old Street and North London courts)[20] have been included because they are known to the writer and have good newspapers which provide generous coverage of local political and industrial developments, and a detailed record of the proceedings of the local courts.[21] Brief sketches of each of them follow to bring out their salient characteristics of size and wealth, industrial and social structure.

The towns vary in size. Barnsley had a population of 68,991 in 1921 and grew thereafter to reach a peak of 75,625 in 1951. A slight decline followed to 75,330 in 1971. Walsall has grown slowly from a population of 96,964 in 1921. It reached 114,514 in 1951 and 117,836 ten years later. Birkenhead has experienced a small loss of population in the fifty years from 1921 (145,592) to 1971 (137,738). Brighton and Hove have expanded from a combined population of 182,321 in 1921 to 225,875 in 1951 and 238,740 twenty years later.

The greatest population changes have taken place in north London. The four LCC boroughs of Hackney, Bethnal Green, Stoke Newington and Shoreditch had a combined population of 495,872 in 1921, and differed greatly in size from one another. Hackney had double the combined populations of Bethnal Green and Shoreditch. During the 1920s and 1930s there was some loss of population as a result of long-overdue slum clearance and re-housing, and the move of some of the better-off sections of the population to the suburbs. The 1939-45 war forced even larger changes as population was driven out by the Blitz and the later bombing campaigns. By 1945 the population was estimated at just under 290,000 – a loss of 200,000 since 1921.

As the blitzed areas were rebuilt, people moved back and by 1951 the combined population had risen to 323,733. During the following decade, however, decline resumed as a result of redevelopment, an increase in the amount of space taken up by industry and commercial developments, and suburbanisation. By 1961 the population had fallen to 304,319.

Important changes had also taken place in the balance between the various north London boroughs. By 1961 Hackney was larger than the other three combined. The greatest loss of population had been suffered by the poorest working-class districts in Shoreditch and Bethnal Green. The population of Shoreditch had fallen from 104,308 in 1921 to 40,465 in 1961 while the decline in Bethnal Green was slightly larger over the same period: from 117,238 to 47,018. The population of Stoke Newington, on the other hand, remained very stable: 52,167 in 1921; 52,280 in 1961.

In the re-organisation of local government which resulted in the establishment of the GLC, Hackney, Shoreditch and Stoke Newington were amalgamated to form the new London Borough of Hackney, while Bethnal Green joined Stepney and Poplar in the new borough of Tower Hamlets. The decline of population, however, continued. Hackney's population had been 257,301 in 1961; by 1969 it was estimated at 238,530.

The relative wealth of these areas is more difficult to measure. There is no historical series indicating urban incomes or standards of living. However, the invaluable study of British towns by Moser and Scott gives a breakdown of the social classes for the provincial towns in 1951 (though not for the London boroughs). Their tables show that Brighton and Hove had the highest proportion of population in social classes I and II: 21 per cent in the former and 35.3 per cent in the latter. Birkenhead had 14.4 per cent in these classes, Walsall 12.6 per cent, and Barnsley 9.8 per cent. The order of towns was reversed with social classes IV and V. Hove had 15.9 per cent in these classes, followed by Brighton (24.1 per cent), Walsall (29.7 per cent), Birkenhead (34.6 per cent) and Barnsley (40.4 per cent).[22]

Rateable values provide a crude measure of relative wealth for the period as a whole, and include information for the London boroughs. Significant changes have taken place, with a widening gap emerging between Brighton and Hove and the rest. In 1921 Hove had a rateable value per head of population of £10 10s 0d and Brighton one of £6 7s 8d. The four London boroughs averaged £6 18s 0d, Birkenhead £6 2s 0d, Barnsley £3 18s 0d, and Walsall £3 16s 0d.

By 1951 the gap between 'north' and 'south' had widened. Hove still 'led' with £16 14s 0d, followed by Brighton at £13 2s 0d. The London boroughs averaged £8 18s 0d though Shoreditch with much industrial property had a rateable value per head of £13 14s 0d.

The 1950s saw accelerating changes. By 1961, Brighton and Hove combined had at £24 4s 0d approximately double the rateable value per head of the other provincial towns.[23]

The average for London was £17 8s 0d varying from £31 4s 0d in Shoreditch to £13 10s 0d in Stoke Newington.

The economies of these towns were very varied in the first half of the twentieth century, though there has been a tendency for the differences between them to lessen since the end of the Second World War. Up to the 1950s Barnsley was overwhelmingly a coal mining town. This industry was in decline during the 1920s but still provided work for 44 per cent of the employed males in 1931. Many miners were on the dole at the time of the census.

The situation deteriorated further in the 1930s, and the jobless figures for Barnsley were higher than those for many towns covered by the Special Areas legislation. (The Special Areas Bill became law in 1935. It provided limited financial assistance for the most depressed areas of Engand, Wales and Scotland. Despite high unemployment neither Birkenhead nor Barnsley was included.) The council made vigorous efforts to diversify the town's industrial base and its campaign had some small successes, but the factor that forced through large-scale change was the war, which sent many companies north in search of safety and furthered the transformation of many depressed urban economies. Wartime shadow factories provided fixed capital and Barnsley council appointed a reconstruction committee whose purpose was to consolidate the gains that had been made. A number of medium-sized firms were drawn to the town (Slazenger's, Blackwood Hodge, Brook Motors, etc.), mainly providing employment for women.

New jobs were also needed for men. By 1951, mining and quarrying employed only 25 per cent of the males and during the following twenty years the industry declined further. In 1965, the NCB proposed to close some thirteen local pits employing 7,000 men. Another ten pits were said to have a 'doubtful' future.

The main growth area was the group of industries ancillary to mining. These originally began trading to supply such items as helmets and lamps for the miners, and expanded by selling similar equipment to other industries. Ceag Ltd, for instance, began production of miners' lamps in 1919 and developed as a manufacturer of a wide range of light bulbs and lamps for the motor industry. Men employed in the manufacture of glass, pottery and bricks rose from 5.9 per cent in 1931 to 14.5 per cent in the sample census of 1971. A further 14.2 per cent worked in the distributive trades and 7 per cent in mechanical engineering. The main employers of women in 1971 were distribution (21.5 per cent) and clothing and footwear (11.5 per cent); by that year women accounted for nearly as many workers as men: 46 per cent of the occupied population. In 1951 there had been nearly twice as many men in work as women.

The modern economic history of Birkenhead has been decisively influenced by the fluctuations in the prosperity of the port. By 1920 there were ten miles of docks with corn and grain warehouses; important flour mills were established nearby to take advantage of them. Lairages were constructed to hold livestock imported into Britain and contained twenty one slaughter houses with a capacity for some 2,000 cattle a day. The pens in the nearby market were large enough to display 22,000 sheep and 6,000 cattle for sale at any one time,[24] while the docks had important railway connections and goods yards to carry imports to the rest of the country. Some 2,306 men had work in the docks in the recession year of 1931.

Birkenhead was also an important shipbuilding centre and at the height of the boom at the end of the First World War employment had reached some 25,000 males. Thereafter a relentless decline ensued and by 1931 the port was in severe crisis and Cammell Laird's was losing money heavily. Only 2,800 men actually had work in shipbuilding and ship repairing at the time of the census.

Sustained recovery began with rearmament and by the late 1930s shipbuilding had revived, but unemployment remained a considerable problem in Birkenhead. The town had declined as a shipping centre and the American trade had been particularly hard-hit by the recession. The more vigorous of Birkenhead's shipping companies re-oriented their business to Australia and the Far East and eight were still operating as late as 1963.

War and post-war demand took the shipbuilding industry to new heights of activity and by 1951 employment rose to

11,800, representing 26 per cent of the town's male labour force. The docks, however, were already in decline, and less than 2,000 men now worked there, while the railways also were unable to sustain traditional levels of employment. The council had long been concerned at Birkenhead's over-dependence on marine industries. A number of growth points had been selected and attempts made to build up the cloth-ing, printing, engineering and brewing industries. This policy had some success but shipbuilding continued to dominate the town's economy, accounting for 27 per cent of the occupied males in the sample census of 1971. The industrial diversifica-tion campaign had had most success in providing work for women. In 1951, 26 per cent of the occupied population had been female; by 1971 the proportion had risen to 34 per cent.

The economy of Brighton was also over-dependent on a single sector for much of our period — leisure. In 1931 51 per cent of the town's women workers and 10 per cent of the men were engaged in personal service which was very vul-nerable to seasonal changes in the level of employment, as was the building industry, the largest employer of men in the town (12 per cent of the males). Brighton had a serious prob-lem of poverty in the 1930s and it was suggested that the town had proportionately as many people living in hardship as the depressed areas. Brighton's neighbour, Hove, had few industries, and had developed mainly as a residential centre catering for commuters to London and the retired.

Brighton's main asset was its location on the south coast within easy travelling distance of the capital, but in the late 1930s this asset became a disadvantage as employers preferred to invest as far away from the possibility of damage by air attack as possible. This blunted the growth of the most promising sector of the local economy, light engineering, which employed just under 12 per cent of the males in 1931, but only 9 per cent in 1951. The Second World War was a disaster for Brighton: the town was a restricted area, it suf-fered some bombing, and its holiday facilities had been neg-lected for over five years. It never regained its pre-eminence as a resort. There was some recovery in the 1950s but the growth in overseas travel limited its extent and the labour force anyway sought to avoid the low pay and dull work associated with the hotel and catering industries. Women in particular wanted an alternative. By 1951 only 14 per cent of women and 5.4 per cent of men were employed in these industries.

The main points of expansion were the distributive trades and professional and scientific services. The town's location was now an unqualified advantage and by 1971, 10 per cent of the men and 23 per cent of the women were employed in professional and scientific services. The distributive trades were also important employers (13.9 per cent of men; 22 per cent of women) but hotels and restaurants provided work for only 3 per cent of males and 5 per cent of females. The twenty years after 1951 saw a substantial rise in the proportion of Brighton's employed female population from 24.5 per cent of the total to 41 per cent.

After the First World War Walsall council had been anxious to demonstrate the precise advantages of its location: 'Here we are, right in the heart of industrial England, but not in the "Black Country" if you please!'[25] Yet it was proximity to the thriving industries of the Black Country that provided the town's economic salvation as its staple trades went into severe decline during the 1920s.

Walsall was eight miles from Birmingham, on the edge of the south Staffordshire coalfield, 'with mines actually inside the borough.' Although the town shared the variety of industries for which the West Midlands was famous, certain sectors predominated: the manufacture of metal products, which accounted for 32 per cent of male workers in 1931 and 21 per cent of the females; and the manufacture of leather and leather goods ('Walsall is *par excellence* the "saddlery" borough').[26] The leather industry was however in serious difficulties as was the town's mining industry and these two accounted for nearly 15 per cent of male employment in 1931.

The saddlery and ancillary trades had been undermined by the rise of the motor trade. In 1916 the town guide had listed 72 firms as engaged in saddlery and related trades; by 1932, 70 per cent of the saddlers had 'nothing to do'.[27]

The recession in leather hit female employment harder than male: nearly 18 per cent of women worked in this industry. In the event, those sections that survived did so by adapting to the requirements of growth industries, and especially motor cars. The 1930s represented the low point for leather and it was able to maintain its position over the following twenty years. In 1951 it provided work for 5.5 per cent of the men and 13.6 per cent of the women.

The real growth sector in Walsall was the metal trades. The town supplied parts for a wide-range of engineering industries — tubes, conduit fittings, mouldings, etc. — as well as domestic hardware and metal smallware. In 1951 metal manufacture and metal goods combined accounted for nearly 30 per cent of the occupied males; by 1971 the proportion had risen to 41.2 per cent. More than 30 per cent of the town's women were also employed in these industries. None the less, employment opportunities for women were poorer in Walsall than in Brighton or Barnsley: in 1971 only 37 per cent of the town's workforce was female.

The industrial structure of the four boroughs of north London was dominated for most of this period by the clothing and furniture industries. Their structure was complex: although both contained a number of large concerns like Canda Manufacturing which employed 1,600 people, they included numerous small firms scattered over many workshops and small factories. Around them gathered many ancillary trades. There was some specialisation in the various boroughs: glass, glue and screws were manufactured in Bethnal Green and veneers and paint in Shoreditch. By the 1950s that borough alone had 1,200 separate firms, most of them employing 20 to 100 workers.

Both clothing and furniture were vulnerable to changes in fashion and to the influence of government policy: they were invariably early targets in any campaign to reduce consumer spending. At the start of the 1930s, with paper and printing, they dominated employment in these boroughs. The manufacture of furniture and fittings was more strongly concentrated in Bethnal Green and Shoreditch, clothing in Hackney, and clothing and printing in Stoke Newington. Clothing was the most important employer of women in the four boroughs in 1931. It provided work for 31 per cent of them, and 9 per cent of the men. Furniture and fittings employed 11.5 per cent of the occupied males and 2 per cent of the females while paper and printing took 6.2 per cent of the men and 8.3 per cent of the women.

The history of these industries during the next twenty years was turbulent but they continued to provide employment for large numbers of people. The furniture industry was badly affected by the depression: during the 1930s it was estimated that 80 per cent of the furniture manufactured in Shoreditch was retailed by hire purchase, which fell victim to the decline in consumer incomes. Housebuilding schemes later in the decade stimulated a revival but the war intervened and the Utility programme imposed severe restrictions on both the furniture and clothing industries. Plant and machinery was badly damaged by the Blitz and flying bomb campaigns, while Utility lowered standards and sacrificed skill and a sense of style to the requirements of cheap mass production. Demand, however, rose throughout the war and any entrepreneur who could obtain illicit materials and labour believed he could sell anything he produced for high prices on the black market.

During the 1930s there had been a tendency for industry to move away from the cramped conditions of north London to new sites in Essex and Hertfordshire and this process was resumed in the late 1940s and 1950s. Employment in clothing and furniture was not greatly reduced by the time of the census of 1951, but both industries lost jobs in the following two decades. They were adversely affected by the cyclical fluctuations in the national economy and especially by the interruptions to production caused by 'stop-go'. By 1971 the biggest employer in the new London borough of Hackney was the distributive trades (15 per cent of the men and 14 per cent of the women). Clothing accounted for 9 per cent of the men and 21 per cent of the women; furniture took 5.7 per cent of the men, and paper and printing 7.3 per cent of them. Women lost most from the decline in these staple industries. In 1931 they accounted for 38 per cent of the occupied labour force in the three London boroughs which later constituted the new borough of Hackney. By 1971 the proportion had risen only marginally to 39 per cent.

The districts of north and east London discussed here are indistinguishable in the police reports for the capital from

areas as different as Hampstead, Chelsea, Kensington and
Westminster. Yet Hackney and the neighbouring boroughs
had the reputation of being the most 'violent' and 'criminal'
in the capital. Hoxton was said to be the 'toughest neighbour-
hood' in east London,[28] its 'main crimes' burglary, shopbreaking and the theft of motor cars. A crime writer in the
1930s claimed it was the only district in London in which
women played a key role. 'Many' of them were 'expert'
burglars and shopbreakers.[29] Bethnal Green was 'known' for
its villains and Hackney itself for cat burglars.[30] Certain
streets like Brick Lane and Flower and Dean Street were held
to be particularly dangerous while Petticoat Lane was said in
the early 1920s to be a 'hot bed' of pickpockets. 'You could
lose your watch or tie at one end, walk through without
missing it, and see it being offered for sale at the other end.'[31]
Cyril Burt thought that districts like Shoreditch in the early
1920s provided 'a strategic base for nefarious designs. The
professional criminal likes to fix his headquarters, not in the
heart of hardworking penury, but on the edge of the richer
haunts of business, pleasure, or residential comfort; at the
same time he feels safer with a wide slum-district at his rear,
where he can lose himself upon occasion, much as Fagin and
Bill Sikes retreated into Whitechapel when the hue and cry
was raised.'[32] Peter Willmott found in his study of adolescent
boys in Bethnal Green in the early 1960s that 'stealing' was
'normal' up to the age of about nineteen or twenty. What
goes on after 'is stealing from or defrauding one's employer
– often dignified by being described as "knocking-off" or
"fiddling". "I stole a table-top from my firm", said an 18
year old, "but I don't call that stealing".'[33]

Birkenhead is situated on the 'left' bank of 'violent, turbulent' Merseyside with its potent dockside mix of immigrants
and their descendents, long regarded as 'one of Britain's
problem areas'.[34] The reports of the chief constable offer a
somewhat different picture. Birkenhead was hit early and
hard by the recession which followed the First World War
yet he was 'pleased to be able to state that in spite of the
distress caused by unemployment . . . there has been no
serious breach of the peace.'[35] Nor was there during the rest
of the decade: conduct continued 'admirable'.[36] In the early

1930s, however, the patience of the unemployed was 'exhausted'. Protests and demonstrations demanding an increase in the PAC[37] scales culminated in severe riots, a 'week-end of whirlwind terror', sixty six injuries and 'thousands of pounds of damage'. When the PAC promised to raise its scales and the council passed a resolution asking the government to abolish the means test, the situation 'calmed down'.[38] During the late 1930s and again in the late 1940s indictable crime rose but successive chief constables argued that given more resources they would be able to cope. The great majority of the people of Birkenhead were 'law-abiding' and 'responsible.'

Brighton has long been described as 'a suburb of the metropolis'; in the 1920s and '30s it was 'a seaside town with a reputation', a 'vulgar' place 'fit only for illicit weekends'.[39] Its reputation for outright criminality was greatly increased by the publication of Graham Greene's novel *Brighton Rock*, with its vivid description of the conflict between the race-boss Colleoni and the peripheral but violent gang led by 'The Boy', Pinkie. Brighton racecourse, like others in the south of England, was indeed a battleground in the 1920s and 30s as racing gangs struggled for supremacy but their impact on the town must not be exaggerated. Gangs fought one another with razors yet the highest number of malicious woundings occurred in 1936, when there were six; in most years in the 1930s there were between one and three. The activities of racing gangs were never mentioned in police reports. Brighton did have a criminal fringe but they turned their attention to quieter, less violent activities. There was an average of thirty frauds a year between 1931 and 1939 while the value of property stolen or embezzled rose by 60 per cent between 1936 and 1938 and by five times between 1938 and 1950.[40]

Statistics of convictions used in this study are based on local newspaper reports of court proceedings. The object is to discover serious instances of black economy activity and all prosecutions of significance would have been picked up by the local newspapers. Indeed press reports for most of this period are comprehensive and include the most minor cases of drunkenness, petty larceny, as well as motoring offences. After 1950, however, minor prosecutions were not necessarily included in reports while newspaper strikes occasionally prevented complete coverage in certain years. These developments will be indicated in the text.

2

The Black Economy during the
First World War, 1914-18

The heart of the black economy during the First World War
was the black market. Between 1915 and 1918 it grew unchecked until it threatened the war effort itself. Civil servants
warned ministers what was happening and drew up schemes
to control the black market, but while Asquith was prime
minister the government shrank from making the required
effort. When Lloyd George took over, policy-making generally
was galvanised but this did not extend to the Ministry of Food
for some time. The new minister was Lord Devonport, a
crony of Lloyd George's. He did not prove adequate to the
task before him. His department was formed in December
1916 but eighteen months passed before it succeeded in
bringing order to the supply of food.

The crux of the difficulty lay in Britain's heavy dependence
on imported foods. Before the war some two-thirds of the
food eaten in Great Britain came from abroad, including four-
fifths of the cereals, two-thirds of the meat, three-quarters
of the fruit and all the sugar (most of that imported from
Germany and Austria-Hungary). After the war started U-boat
campaigns increasingly disrupted supplies. The British har-
vest of 1916 was poor while Canada and the USA suffered
their worst harvests for twenty years. As domestic demand
held up and the troops at the front had also to be fed, prices
rose sharply. The cost of a four pound loaf doubled compared to 1914. Meat prices rose with 'peculiar speed' during
1917 and supplies disappeared 'catastrophically'[1] at the start
of the following year. That winter severe shortages of tea,
margarine and sugar developed. Goods vanished from the
shops (or went 'under the counter') and queuing became
part of daily life. Nineteen-seventeen was the worst year of

the war and public anxiety focused particularly on food. Wild rumours spread and people panicked. Housewives queued for hours: husbands left factories and children schools to take their turn.

'In practically all the well-known shopping centres in London on Saturday the supplies of meat were exhausted long before the queues were half-served . . . Hundreds of homes — more likely the number ran into thousands — were also without butter or margarine on Saturday . . . Queues in all parts of the metropolis gathered as early as 5 a.m. It would be idle to assert that these long lines of people to be seen in almost every big thoroughfare were cheerful and content . . . In two instances off Tottenham Court Road, where the supply gave out while the queue was still long, the police were called to disperse an angry crowd . . .'[2] In Brighton in the same month 'pork was unprocurable . . . only scraps of bacon could be picked up at the shops. There was a run on fish . . . An enforced vegetarian diet was a common experience . . .'[3] The shortages did not only affect food: in early 1917 coal had vanished from the merchants' stores. 'I have never seen anything quite so dreadful', a London councillor wrote, 'as this daily clamouring for coal. It is a real tragedy. Old women, sick women and little children have to jostle round the doors of the wharves to get coal — pleading for the privilege of paying for it with ready cash . . . Something will have to be done soon.'[4]

About the same time vans carrying potatoes in London were attacked and plundered. Police tried to defuse tense situations by 'persuading' owners to sell potatoes to the crowds.[5] Queues up to a mile long formed outside butchers' and grocers' shops. People wrote letters describing what was happening to their relatives at the front, causing 'unrest' in the trenches.[6] Increasingly vigorous calls were made for the resignation of the minister.

Lord Devonport had seemed to be well qualified for the post: he was one of the founders of the company that eventually became International Stores and was known as 'a successful pioneer of the modern chain store system'.[7] This may in fact have been a handicap because he continued to think like a store-owner after he became minister. He refused to accept that voluntary principles would not work in war-time. Controls meant curtailing the traditional freedoms of the retailer, ending competition and 'charging what the market would bear'. Lord Devenport persisted in advocating voluntarism but when this system was applied to rations it had 'no scientific basis and bore no relation to the facts of life' for most of the population. Working-class families had not traditionally bought much meat; their diet depended on large quantities of bread. Devenport allowed them two and a half pounds of meat a week each, far more than they could afford, but only four pounds of bread. Many working people ate as much as ten or even fourteen pounds of bread a week.[8]

Food policy failed most seriously with sugar. The Ministry of Food did not compel retailers to distribute supplies fairly among their customers and many began to impose a 'condition of sale'. They would not sell sugar unless the shopper bought something else. The poor suffered most of all from this as hordes of middle-class housewives descended on shops in working-class areas. They bought up most of the sugar and many other goods as well.

The authorities were very slow to grasp the seriousness of this. As late as 1916 the Sugar Commission regarded the imposition of conditions of sale 'favourably' while the Chancellor of the Exchequer, Reginald McKenna, also gave the practice limited approval.[9] By March 1917 Devonport had been forced to prohibit conditions of sale but as he also failed to introduce rationing the shortages were made even worse. One local newspaper noted that 'when it was announced that an order had been made forbidding the tradesmen making the sale of sugar conditional on the purchase of other goods, the public innocently believed that all they had to do in future was to walk into a shop, ask for the sugar they wanted and receive it, and, if the shopman insisted on other purchases, call a policeman. But they were reckoning without their hosts . . . there is no law that can compel a shopkeeper to supply sugar if he doesn't want to, even though he may have an ample stock . . .'[10]

A similar error was made when Devonport attempted to control the price of potatoes. He fixed a maximum price but did not commandeer supplies. Potatoes vanished from the legitimate to the black market.

He finally resigned at the end of May 1917, 'a disappointment and a failure.'[11] His successor was Lord Rhondda, a
dynamic coal magnate. During his brief period in office the
slow progress of the Ministry of Food towards the introduction of rationing on the basis of a central register of individuals was abandoned and coupon rationing with the shopkeeper introduced. Some local authorities had already anticipated this: Rhondda made the system 'national in extent
and uniformity'[12] but retained a degree of local responsibility
by having it administered by autonomous local committees.
This scheme had three principal features: individual ration
books were issued; customers were tied to certain retailers;
and each retailer was guaranteed a sufficient supply of food
to meet the requirements of his customers. Crucial to the
success of rationing was the strong organisation that backed
it up: government control ensured the certainty of supply.
Once the system was in full operation there was no possibility of a customer going into his local shop with a coupon
and being disappointed. Queues disappeared and foodstuffs
were restored to all tables. William Beveridge claimed that
rationing was 'fair' to rich and poor alike, with supplies of
'good' and 'indifferent' meat (none of it seems actually to
have been 'bad') equally distributed to 'rich' and 'poor' districts.[13] In fact rationing in the First World War meant that
no-one starved; it did not mean that those with money could
not buy their way round the regulations. The rich did not
suffer, as they would have done if their rations had really
been 'equal' to those of the poor.

The logic of government intervention in the economy on
this kind of scale was that controls would have the force of
law. This presented a novel challenge to the local food control
committees, the police and the courts. By no means all of
them were ready to accept it. *The National Food Journal*,
published by the Ministry of Food, kept a record of convictions for black market and related offences. This shows that
the numbers fined or imprisoned for serious[14] offences were
nowhere large. While the war lasted Nottingham had six such
cases, Cardiff four and Southampton three. Plymouth had
none while Leeds, Bradford, Stoke-on-Trent, Portsmouth and
Salford had one each. Among smaller towns, Spalding had

six, Wisbech five and Hove three. These figures do not reflect regional differences in the extent of black marketeering; they measure the willingness of the authorities to accept that 'the market' was now a fit province for the attention of the law and to take infringements of the controls as seriously as other forms of crime. Not all courts were prepared to do so, especially in the provinces. Local businessmen sat on the bench in many towns, as did retailers and wholesalers.

In London the magistrates were stipendiaries. In the early stages of rationing some of them were reluctant to impose any punishment on convicted offenders. T.C.H. Hedderwick at North London court bound over five of the first seven defendants who appeared before him. They were prosecuted for overcharging and all pleaded guilty. He fined the other two 21s 0d and 7s 6d.[15] This was in August 1917, a time of rising social discontent. That winter magistrates sentenced more severely. In December Hedderwick fined a shopkeeper who overcharged £50 while at Old Street court, Clarke Hall began to imprison black market offenders.[16]

At the same time, the government's commitment to local control allowed contrasts to emerge in the policies pursued by the local food committees. By the end of January 1918, Hackney, Bethnal Green, and Shoreditch committees had all taken black marketeers to court but Stoke Newington had not done so. Such differences were noted. Protest meetings drew attention to the fact that members of food control committees had themselves been prosecuted for 'profiteering' and demanded that these committees open their proceedings to public scrutiny.[17] Islington Labour party complained to the Food Controller that they were 'seriously hampered in their endeavour to protect the public from fraudulent practices on the part of food retailers by reason of the inadequate fines inflicted by magistrates'.[18] The Controller replied that he did not have the power to interfere with the courts: it was necessary to rely on the pressure of public opinion and their own view of the seriousness of the situation to bring magistrates to a sterner view of these matters. There were marked variations in the extent to which they did so. Black marketeers fared worse at some courts than others. At Old Street, twenty-seven were fined

£50 or more or jailed while the war lasted, compared to four at North London. At Thames court eleven suffered such penalties, at Marylebone six and at Tower Bridge three. Contrasts in sentencing are inherent in the system. With economic crime it might have been fairer and more efficient to devise a new system, perhaps of tribunals, but this was not seriously considered. The individual magistrate or judge continued to be in charge.

The queues and riots of 1917 and early 1918 had alerted the government to the importance of food policy. When Lord Rhondda died in July 1918 the Labour MP J.R. Clynes was appointed minister. The department itself now took over the initiation of prosecutions in 'recalcitrant' districts. Retailers organised to defend themselves and endeavoured to make their point of view known through the press. 'Why should the retail tradesman be considered the skunk?' the Mayor of Stoke Newington, himself a retailer, demanded. 'The government want to make a scapegoat of somebody, and it seems to me the retail tradesman has to be that scapegoat.'[19]

Retailers were not the only ones to feel they had been picked out unfairly. Wealthy people had anticipated wartime shortages by building up stocks of food and drink. During 1917 such people were stigmatised in press and parliament as 'hoarders' and a campaign was launched to bring them to justice. The government hoped it would thereby demonstrate that it was serious about securing 'equal shares' in wartime. The campaign had something of the emotional atmosphere of a 'moral panic' in which the authorities were determined to discover and make examples, preferably of minor public figures. Many of the 'hoards' had been bought before hoarding became an offence and several of the people prosecuted were arrested when they were trying to get rid of their stockpiles before they came to the notice of the police. Among those convicted were the novelist Marie Corelli (fined £50), the headmaster of a minor public school (fined £50), an Irish MP, and several company directors. In the autumn of 1917 the home of a Walsall metal refiner was raided by police. They found some two thousand pounds of food including nine sacks of potatoes, 126 lbs of sugar, and ten dozen tins of tomatoes. The metal refiner claimed he had bought the food to make Christmas presents to his employees and the poor and his parish priest came to court to support him. Unfortunately he had taken the precaution of hiding the food 'in a recess in the cellar, concealed by a wall which had been built up and carefully whitewashed so as to resemble other parts of the wall'. The prosecuting counsel made great play of the 'exceedingly grave character' of this but a curious ambiguity also emerged in the way he presented his case. A large quantity of liquor had been found in the house but he pointed out that 'many men were in the habit of keeping a little cellar, and were entitled to do so'. The chairman of the bench took the point and observed that 'it was generally understood that a man was entitled to keep a little cellar'. He ruled that the food was to be forfeited but made a 'liberal allowance' of the wine and spirits. The metal refiner was jailed for six months. He decided to appeal and secured the distinguished barrister Edward Marshall Hall to represent him. Marshall Hall made a forceful case and persuaded the court that his client had not hoarded for his own benefit: he really did wish to help the poor. The jail sentence was remitted though the fine of £50 stood. Marshall Hall had also drawn the court's attention to the circumstances in which the hoard had been discovered. The police had received 'information' and had gone to the house while the metal refiner and his wife were away. The source of the information had not been disclosed but it may have crossed the minds of some of the people in court that the possibility of such prosecutions gave dissatisfied servants considerable power.[20]

Hoarders were treated more leniently than their lower-class equivalents, people who tried to get more than their 'fair share' by obtaining two (or more) ration books. Although logic might seem to demand that the rich be jailed and the poor fined, it was the ration card offenders who usually went inside. Seven of them were imprisoned in a single month of 1918. Only four hoarders out of thirty six prosecuted for serious offences were jailed and the sentence on three of these was quashed on appeal.[21] Among them was a hoarder whose 'corridors and bedrooms were invaded' by a store of food; another answered an enquiry from the food office: 'he was not responsible for housekeeping, his time being occupied in building ships as fast as possible to save the country from disaster.'[22] These men were fined whereas Alfred Adams who obtained three rations of sugar was jailed for six weeks, and a woman who secured a second ration book (she had five children) was imprisoned for a month.

The success of the appeals the hoarders had made against their sentences seems to have inhibited the authorities from initiating many similar prosecutions: only three more serious [23] offenders were convicted while the war lasted (two in May and one in July 1918). The attack on hoarders made little difference to the supply of goods — only rationing and controls could do that — and it is unlikely that it satisfied the public demand for fair shares. But the government decided it was necessary to continue this type of inquiry and the hotel trade was investigated next.

During the later stages of the war many wealthy people left their homes and moved into hotels. There they would not have to cope with the problem of finding domestic staff or be obliged to endure their own cooking. The more expensive hotels soon acquired a reputation for luxurious living and they began to come under official scrutiny in early 1918. Between February and July 1918 fifteen hotels were prosecuted. Several were in the West End,[24] others were in provincial cities like Glasgow and Newcastle, still others in seaside resorts such as Worthing, Southport and Brighton.

In early 1918 the panic about meat shortages was at its height. Brighton newspapers recorded 'meatless' weeks in January and commented on the dissatisfaction in the town: people who spent hours queueing and then received nothing were 'not likely to forget the experience'.[25] At the same time local people complained that Londoners had descended on Brighton's seafront hotels where they entertained lavishly. Hotel staff confirmed what was happening. Local branches of the trades unions and the Labour Party took notice. The press picked up the story. Brighton Hotels Association became sufficiently alarmed to pass a resolution against 'the inaccurate statements made by various persons in the town which have the effect of stirring up class hatred and of occasioning damage to the hotel business'. They protested that their consumption of meat was 'below the average of the town' and insisted their guests and staff had had to 'go short'.[26] These claims were very soon put to the test.

At the start of February the manageress of a large seafront hotel was summonsed. When they were added up correctly the hotel's own records showed that, far from going short of meat, an excess of 800 lbs had been used during five weeks at the end of 1917. 'I had no idea we were using so much,' the manageress said. 'But people grumble so much and send up their plates for more that I have sometimes said, "Oh, let them have it for the sake of peace and quietness."'[27] Two similar prosecutions followed. Evidence was based on the hotels' own books and in one case the hotelier was shown to have been using double the amount of meat to which he was entitled. Like the other defendants he blamed his customers for encouraging him to break the law. Guests at the Renata Hotel tipped waiters to bring them extra portions: the hotel management was obliged to watch its own staff like 'a cat watches a mouse'.[28] The fines courts imposed could hardly have done much damage to the hotels' profits: £175 in the first case and £100 in the second. In the third the police officer in charge of the investigation told the court that the hotelier had already been warned on 'several' occasions and had given him 'more trouble than anyone else in the town'.[29] The outcome was a £90 fine. The holiday trade was, after all, the principal business of Brighton and hoteliers were among the town's leading citizens.

The great majority of serious black market convictions followed fairly straightforward cases of overcharging. The pattern of prosecutions in the last fourteen months of the war shows that the authorities concentrated on goods about which public anxiety was greatest. Seven of the first eight attacked 'profiteering' in potatoes. From the spring of 1917 restaurants and cafés in the working-class districts of London ceased to serve potatoes with meals and the shortage soon had 'knock-on' effects on the price of other vegetables. Swedes for instance doubled in price in a single week.[30] Retailers denounced the sale of potatoes to hotels when they themselves could not obtain supplies, while 'wholesale profiteers' and 'middlemen' became the targets of protest meetings and debates in borough councils.[31]

The result was a series of court cases in which 'speculators' were arraigned and fined, sometimes very heavily. The prosecution of a Lincolnshire farmer who had carried out 'numerous and extensive transactions' on the black market was widely reported. He admitted making illegal profits of £4,620 and was fined £6,000 in September 1917.[32] Such penalties did not stop shortages, controls did that, but they may have made black marketeers cautious. The chance of a jail sentence would have made them even more so, but courts did not imprison offenders very often during the First World War. Only 290 were fined £50 or more while the war lasted: 67 between November 1917 and January 1918, 99 between February and April, 61 between May and July, and 63 from August to October. The products mentioned in charges varied as follows:[33]

	potatoes	*sugar*	*milk &* *butter*	*meat &* *poultry*
November 1917 to January 1918	12	10	8	9
February 1918 to April 1918	1	6	21	18
May 1918 to July 1918	0	4	6	28
August 1918 to October 1918	0	2	13	29

Thus during 1918 black markets in potatoes fell away, as did those in sugar. They fluctuated in milk and butter and increased in meat and poultry. Sir William Beveridge thought that the rationing of meat in February 1918 was 'an immediate and almost unqualified success'.[34] The ration was more than enough for most working-class families but it did not match the appetites of the better-off. Retailers knew they could sell meat 'under the counter' to wealthy customers; the difficulty was avoiding getting caught. Wholesalers provided illegal supplies and charged for them: an excess of 100 per cent was common. When they were arrested some offenders admitted frankly what they had been doing. A 'profiteer' in potatoes said, 'don't think I wish you to believe that I did not know I was doing wrong. We all knew it and those who have come and begged me for potatoes at any price knew it. But what could I do? You might take out 500 summonses.'[35] Others tried to buy their way out of the difficulty. A wholesale meat dealer in the East End offered the food control inspector who caught him £50 and so much a week for the next twelve months if he would keep the matter quiet.[36] A baker, also in the East End, tried more drastic action. Questioned by policemen he attacked them and his son joined in. That battle lost, he tried offering a bribe. He was jailed (though for only fourteen days) and his son fined.[37] Other tradesmen tried subtler methods. They paid 'spies' to keep a watch for food inspectors.[38] Few seem to have been as fatalistic as the butcher who put up a collection box in his shop for donations to pay fines.[39]

What do prosecutions reveal about the scale of the black market in the First World War? *The National Food Journal* recorded 290 serious cases but only three of them were prosecutions of black marketeers who had been operating on some scale. One was a sugar factor who supplied customers with over 70,000 tons of sugar without having obtained the necessary permits, and the others were butchers in Marylebone and Manchester who bought meat in excess of their allowances.[40] Most of the rest were shopkeepers who repeatedly overcharged or broke the rationing regulations. They had some local effect but were not in any way attempts to disrupt 'the market' itself. Some black marketeers may have managed to avoid prosecution but it is unlikely there were many of them, given the battery of wartime controls and the determination of the authorities to seek out and prosecute offenders. The numerous small-scale transactions that took place were not collectively large enough to threaten the supply of any product once controls had been introduced. There was nothing in Britain to match the situation in Germany in the later stages of the war. There 'unscrupulous traders took advantage of the general state of want to place on the market an almost inexhaustible variety of worthless substitute foods whose only resemblance to the genuine article was their shape and colour.' By March 1918 some 11,000 substitute foods of this kind were on the market. Indeed, 'large sections of the population were compelled, at least in so far as their means allowed, to supplement their rations by buying on the black market'. Prices in Germany rose for some goods as much as ten times above the pre-war level, whereas in Britain only sugar increased in price so much as three times compared to pre-war.[41]

Most courts imposed lenient punishments. Only thirteen black marketeers were jailed during the last year of the war and only seven were fined more than £500. Another twenty were fined over £200. London magistrates jailed eight of the thirteen. When a shopkeeper was accused of overcharging he replied, 'it is my shop, my margarine, and I shall do what I like with it.' The stipendiary magistrate retorted that 'at the present time tradesmen were simply trustees of public property' and imprisoned the man for six weeks.[42] Provincial benches tended to see the issue less clearly, their vision blurred by the local network of business, political and social relationships, especially when friends or colleagues, fellow parishioners or freemasons appeared in the dock. When the sugar crisis was at its height in the winter of 1917-18 'the grocer's formula of "no sugar" . . . reached the rank of the "not at home" formula as a recognised but unchallengable lie.'[43] Hove Food Control Committee decided that action must be taken about this. They employed a retired police inspector to make enquiries. He visited a number of shops whose owners had put in claims for sugar, saying they had none. In two he found stocks of sugar. One man had a hundredweight in his shop but had entered 'nil' on the claim form. 'An oversight!' he protested. The court fined both men £2.[44]

In provincial towns, the stigma of appearing in court and having the case written up in the local press may have been sufficient to deter offenders from breaking the law again. One of the Hove defendants was indeed 'much affected' by his appearance in the dock. In London and perhaps also in the great provincial cities the pressure of public disgrace was not so strong. Black marketeers had often had several brushes with the law. Of twenty-four serious offenders convicted at Old Street in the last year of the war, nine had previous convictions. One had been prosecuted four times and another three. Four more were said by police to have offered them bribes. Several had falsified their books, hidden black market supplies in unhygienic conditions (1,400 lbs of sugar in a cellar 'covered with sacks, old clothes and rubbish'), or had sold adulterated food. Two had given the police information about black marketeering by neighbouring shopkeepers.

Courts sometimes singled out those whose surnames indicated they were of European extraction; 'The defendants would find that the English police were not to be bribed by Russian Jews';[45] nor were Welshmen spared. 'I have remarked lately on the number of Welshmen charged with adulteration of milk. If it is not a Morgan it is a Jones, if it is not a Jones it is a Jenkins. With the appearance of an arch-druid you seem to be an arch-adulterator.'[46]

Nonetheless fines of £50 or over were the exception, even in London. In 1918 some 28,657 black market prosecutions were initiated in England, Scotland and Wales, England accounting for 24,296 of them. The percentage of convictions was high: 92.1 per cent in England, 95.8 per cent in Scotland and 87.8 per cent in Wales. Average fines were small: £4 16s 4d in Wales, £4 8s 4d in England and £3 5s 3d in Scotland.[47] So Lillian Beckwith need not have worried too much. Her father was a shopkeeper in a town near Liverpool. When he received a delivery of bacon he

> took his sharpest knife and pared off small pieces of rind which bore the blue stamp branding it as 'Swedish', which had been explained to me as being necessary because our customers believed they were buying 'Danish' bacon and he was afraid one or two of them might be astute enough to notice that 'Danish' bacon bore red stamp marks. I was shocked at first to discover that Father, who punished me for cheating or telling lies, should be capable of doing so himself, but I soon grew used to such deceptions as being part of normal shopkeeping practice. When Father handed me a damp cloth and a packet of 'Vim' and instructed me to rub the 'Irish' stamp off a consignment of eggs so that they could be sold as 'fresh' my only reaction was fear that Father might be found out and put in prison.[48]

Black markets need to be supplied. Goods came from illicit sources. Were many stolen? If we compare the pattern of higher value thefts (those in which at least £100 worth of goods were stolen) for 1913, the last full year of peace, and 1917, when the repercussions of 'total war' were reverberating throughout the economy, there is not much evidence that the black market was a significant influence. In Birkenhead, Barnsley and Walsall there were no such thefts in either year. In Brighton there was one in 1913 (jewellery valued by the owner at £170) and one in 1917 (army clothing worth £249). In north London there were eight thefts in 1913 and seventeen in 1917. In four of the eight jewellery was taken and cloth or clothing in three. In those horse-and-carriage days thieves were easily follcwed and a policeman on a bicycle arrested two of them. Two others were caught in the act. Only one robbery was carried out by a group of 'professional' criminals. Jewellery worth £117,000 was stolen in transit between Paris and London by men themselves in the jewellery business, though two of them had records. They became the object of a frantic police search and all were caught. It appears that they attempted to influence the verdict at their trial by having an associate send a threatening letter to a juryman: he handed the letter to the judge. Sentences of five and seven years were imposed.[49]

Only one theft in 1913 fed directly into the black economy. Alfred Watts, a pawnbroker's manager, stole jewellery worth £250 from his employer, a pawnbroking partnership with twenty one branches in the capital. Police claimed he had been building up a toy shop with the firm's takings; the magistrate jailed him for six months.[50]

In 1917 there were nine thefts of cloth or clothing. Property taken included rolls of silk (£4,000 worth; the owner offered £200 for information); boots and shoes (they were later spotted on a street trader's stall by the owner and recovered); 600 Panama hats (the thief sold them for 10d a dozen; the manufacturer's sale value was 5s each); cotton goods, drapery and furs. Five thefts took place at warehouses (there had not been any in 1913). In 1917 jewellery was stolen in four instances but three of these were carried out by the same man. He obtained entry to the private homes of wealthy people by pretending to be an insurance assessor.[51] Goods in transit were slightly more vulnerable in 1917. Four vans were taken compared to one in 1913. The Commissioner of the Metropolitan Police summed up in his report for 1918 and 1919: 'Certain classes of crime against property ... show a considerable increase'; shopbreaking in particular was 'much more common' than in 1913. He attributed an influence on these developments to the 'high value of certain commodities'.[52]

The influence of the black market on patterns of theft from the employer is even less clear. If 1913 and 1917 are compared the number of people aged eighteen and over convicted in Barnsley and Walsall 'fell' while in the other two it 'rose'.[53] At Old Street and North London courts the number convicted 'rose' from sixteen in 1913 to thirty seven in 1917. Such figures are, however, more revealing of the attitudes and policies of the authorities (who include employers as well as the police and the courts in this category of crime) than a measure of the amount of pilfering actually taking place.

Employers varied greatly in the policy they followed with respect to pilfering. The railway companies seem invariably to have taken offenders to court. In 1913 five out of seven convictions in Barnsley, and four out of sixteen in Walsall, were of railway employees. In both towns, inquiries began because of 'constant pilferings' (Barnsley) or 'wholesale thefts' (Walsall).[54] Employers in the docks and shipyards also took a tough line with pilferers and in Birkenhead thirteen of the sixteen convicted in 1913 were dockers or shipyard workers. Employers instructed counsel to press charges strongly in court. Thus Anchor Line in 1913: 'scarcely a ship left the port without some part of the cargo being tampered with, and the foreign agents were continually making claims for breach of contract and damage to goods'.[55] Cammell Laird's pointed out in 1917: 'They had a lot of pilfering. They asked the Bench to inflict such punishment as would be a deterrent to further theft.'[56]

In Brighton, too, one group of employers, the hoteliers, accounted for five of the seven prosecutions in 1913, while in 1917 four of the people convicted were railway workers and four hotel employees. In Birkenhead in 1917 fifteen of the thirty two persons convicted were dock and shipyard workers and ten were railwaymen, while in Walsall seven of the eight were railwaymen. It should not therefore be concluded that pilfering 'rose' in Birkenhead and Brighton and 'fell' in Walsall. Changes and contrasts in company policy could make all the difference, as could the decision to investigate a certain dock or goods yard one year but not another.

Courts also varied in their response to pilfering. Although the quantities of goods stolen at the railway stations in Barnsley and Walsall in 1913 did not differ greatly in value and none of the men had been caught before, the Barnsley pilferers were put on probation for twelve months while those in Walsall were fined from £3 to £10 (their average wage was £1 3s 0d a week).[57]

Brighton hotel staff were perhaps the most unlucky. They had taken trivial quantities of goods (six towels, seven spoons etc.) but all were jailed. Two of them went inside for three months for first offences. These were Britons; the others were Europeans. They were recommended for deportation. In 1917 two of the four hotel employees were jailed and two fined: one of them £5 for stealing 6s worth of goods from the Hotel Metropole. 'Is that not rather steep?' he asked the magistrate. 'Instead of thinking it steep you should consider yourself lucky in not having been sent to jail,' was the reply. But the question hints that pilfering was common in hotels and not often punished by prosecution. In another Brighton case the defence pleaded that 'in 99 cases out of 100 such small things' as the defendant 'had taken were generally recognised as the perquisites of chefs'.[58] Those prosecuted may in fact have failed to satisfy management in other ways — though nothing was said about this in court.

Most pilferers stole metals in 1913 and food in 1917 but the number of pilferers convicted was so small that not too much should be made of this.[59] Company policy on theft from the employer may have been the decisive influence. Clothing companies tended to prosecute offenders when they caught them. Achille Serre explained in 1913 that 'robberies had been so terrible that his firm felt it imperative to make an example of the prisoner.'[60] In 1916-17 the firm claimed to have lost a garment for every worker it employed.[61] Laundries also prosecuted pilferers when they caught them. Four did so in 1917 and gave one magistrate the impression that their establishments were 'dens of thieves'. 'There are more thieves in laundries', he complained on another occasion, than anywhere else and jailed offenders who appeared before him.[62] Yet laundries were obliged to recompense their customers for clothes lost and they had also to account to their insurers. Hence they felt it necessary to prosecute pilferers where other firms might be content to warn or dismiss them.

Few of the goods stolen found their way into the black market. In 1913 a young man took loads of bricks belonging to his employer and sold them to a firm of builders. When they received 'information' about this the police made enquiries and learned that he had been selling them for 15s a thousand.[63] There were no similar thefts in north London in 1917 and only one in Birkenhead. There three Great Western railwaymen 'took a heterogeneous collection of articles which would have well nigh stocked a small general dealer's shop'. They tried to sell several hundred packets of tea, soap and margarine. All were jailed.[64] In Brighton soldiers at two army camps sold goods to local dealers and pawnbrokers. One of these had a contract to collect refuse from Preston Barracks. Soldiers concealed goods from the quartermaster's stores in his van. The police had 'suspected' him for some time but only began to watch the barracks when they received an anonymous letter. He was jailed but none of the solders was prosecuted. In the other case the defendant claimed that 'it was more or less an open thing for buying and selling to go on' at the base.[65]

The great majority of the sixty two people convicted in 1913 stole small quantities for their own use. Only four were proved to have sold the goods they stole. In 1917 six did so. There was some stiffening in sentencing in Birkenhead in 1917 but not elsewhere.

In 1913 Birkenhead magistrates had usually imposed small fines. Two men were jailed for a month; thirteen fined £1 or less. In the remaining case Anchor Line, the prosecutor, asked the magistrates to impose a stern sentence on an employee who had stolen a roll of cloth 97½ yards long. The fine was £2.[66]

In 1917 twelve pilferers out of thirty two were jailed. Thomas Basnett took two bottles of brandy worth 15s and was imprisoned for a month; John Flynn was caught drinking whisky on a boat and went inside for twenty one days; Joseph Milligan sold a stolen bottle of whisky worth 7s 6d for 6s 6d (two months hard labour); Charles Holmes 'engaged as a watchman on the ship for the very purpose of preventing pilfering' was questioned by police because his 'pockets were very bulky'. Cigarettes worth £1 10s 0d were found and he went to jail for a month. PC Martin Hughes, with fifteen years in the force, was much luckier. He 'asked' one docker for raisins and another for sugar and was given both. Inspector Birch searched him when he was leaving the dock. The bench took the policeman's 'excellent previous character into account' when they fined him £5.[67]

In north London just under half the pilferers were jailed in both years. In 1913 no employer had spoken up for a worker in court but in 1917 six did so. One succeeded in persuading the magistrate to remit a sentence of imprisonment by praising the 'character' of the pilferer; another told the court the man 'had a very good character'; a third informed an employee in the dock that he would not be sacked. These three pilferers had been arrested away from the workplace. In other prosecutions employers regretted they had to bring charges but said the reason was the rise in pilfering at their firm. They wanted to 'warn' the other employees. In 1913 only one gave this explanation but in 1917 seven did so. 'Losses' were 'serious' and 'continuous'; 'more serious than ever before'; 'an ever-growing nuisance.'[68] These contradictory trends in employers' statements may indicate that there was a real rise in pilfering in 1917 but that they were very reluctant to sack workers because of the difficulty of replacing them at a time of acute labour shortage. However, the numbers are too few to draw more than the most tentative conclusions.

The black economy during the First World War revolved around the black market. Many wholesalers and retailers traded illegally, uninhibited by the patriotic appeals of wartime. They included companies of some size and supposed reputation. Among those convicted were Home and Colonial Stores, Lipton's, W.H. Cullen (one branch of this company was prosecuted twelve times during the war),[69] the Ritz, the

Carlton Club, and seven co-operative societies in various parts of the country, including those in Sheffield, Swansea and Peterborough. The war revealed how the retail trades were habitually prepared to flout the law. Their business practices needed investigating but parliament missed the opportunity. The problem would re-emerge during the Second World War.

Penalties courts imposed were almost always lenient. Sir William Beveridge claimed that 'trivial fines' were 'not the order of the day' and gave as an instance the fine of £5,500 imposed on a farmer who had systematically overcharged in September 1917.[70] But fines of that size were very unusual; courts seem to have relied on the shame of an appearance in court and the press notoriety that followed to deter offenders. There is indeed little evidence of major dealing in the black market once controls had been introduced. It is unlikely that many 'big operators' escaped the scrutiny of the authorities in the last year of the war. Britain managed to avoid the fate of her enemies. In Germany there was a 'tremendous expansion of the black market . . . large sections of the population were compelled, at least in so far as their means allowed, to supplement their rations by buying on the black market.'[71] According to 'reliable' estimates in 1918 one-quarter to one-third of milk, butter and cheese production and one-third to one-half of egg, meat and fruit production passed through the hands of black marketeers at prices up to ten times the peacetime price. Nothing in Britain resembled this.

The Black Economy between the Wars, 1919-39

The interwar years in Britain are often remembered as years of widespread unemployment and poverty. The end of the war was followed by a brief boom which broke in 1920. Unemployment soon passed the million mark. The Wall Street crash and the ensuing world depression drove unemployment even higher: the official figures showed a British peak of around three million in January 1933. Britain's export industries were hard hit by the recession: coal, shipbuilding and textiles contracted severely. The consumer industries of the capital did not escape. Clothing, printing and publishing, and the manufacture of furniture all suffered. Many businessmen had to struggle to survive; the workers felt the pressure in their pay packets.

When the First World War ended, the authorities believed that the economic danger had ended with it and that they could relax. But shortages did not cease with the fighting, prices continued to rise, workers made pay-claims and justified them by pointing to inflation, profiteering and the black market. During the first half of 1919 controls had to be reinforced and even extended. The Ministry of Food was not abolished until nearly three years after the war finished.

J.R. Clynes resigned as minister when Labour withdrew from the coalition. He was succeeded by a Labour coalitionist, George Roberts. This change at the top contributed to the mood of uncertainty at the ministry. Some local food committees were anxious to lay down their responsibilities now the war was over but others were determined to keep enforcing the law. Black marketeers took advantage of the confusion; popular dissatisfaction grew. *The National Food Journal* noted that in some areas in the first half of 1919 'offenders were dealt with so leniently as to make the penalty imposed useless as a deterrent.' As industrial turbulence grew during the year a general 'tightening up' took place and the situation was said to have 'improved'.[1] But the response was patchy. From the end of the war to June 1920 there were twelve convictions for serious black market offences in Birmingham, eleven in Liverpool, ten each in Glasgow and Manchester, but only one in Sheffield and one in Leeds. Croydon had one case and Brighton two whilst small towns like Rugby had six and Leigh five.

During the war courts had been reluctant to jail black marketeers; after it was over they invariably imposed fines. The British and Argentine Meat Company was a frequent offender. In December 1918 it was found to have fraudulently secured £24,000 worth of meat in a space of three months. The company was fined £150. A Woking butcher found guilty of selling 8,000 lbs of meat off the ration was fined £175 in May 1919. A Nottingham cattle dealer who slaughtered 166 head of cattle for sale to the black market was fined £450: his profit (£710) more than covered it. When the directors of Cinderford Co-operative Society in the Forest of Dean were asked to produce their books they destroyed them and admitted the fact in court (fined £147). A pig dealer who disposed of over 9,000 animals to the black market in Sheffield was fined £918. And so on. Ration card offenders, however, did not benefit from the softening in sentencing. They continued to go to jail, even during January and February 1919 when the relaxation of controls upon retailers and wholesalers was at its greatest. Maud Ellison of Birkenhead, who had retained the ration books of two of her lodgers who had left and used them to help feed her household of three, was jailed for two months.[2] The British and Argentine Meat Company was involved in seven court cases in 1918 and 1919 in places as far apart as Glasgow and Cardiff, Paddington and Manchester. Four concerned overcharging and two selling adulterated food. The company was fined a total of £626.

Courts often distinguished between black marketeers and their 'servants'. The former were usually fined and the latter jailed. In October 1919 a butcher's manager who overcharged for meat was jailed for twenty one days; his employer was fined £50.[3] 'Personally,' said the owner of four shops in another prosecution, 'he had no knowledge of these particular [black market] transactions.' The magistrate retorted that a man 'making large sums of money would know the prices at which his goods were sold.'[4] But such a clear allocation of responsibility was unusual.

Distinctions in sentencing between 'master' and 'servant' were paralleled by continuing disparities between districts. In March 1919 a West Bromwich butcher was jailed for four months because he slaughtered cattle for sale to the black market. In the same month a Loughborough butcher with twenty-two previous convictions for similar offences was fined £124 for doing the same thing.[5] The British court system continued to be a blunt instrument for dealing with economic crimes.

During 1919 the resumption of normal shipping patterns permitted the government to end rationing on some products. Margarine was freed in February, jam in April, beef and mutton in December. Sugar was the last food to be taken off the ration in November 1920. Black marketeers showed most interest in 1919 in meat, poultry and alcohol:[6] the most common offence was overcharging. Among the firms 'caught out' were Selfridge's, the Royal Arsenal Co-operative (twice) and Lipton's. The number of prosecutions for selling adulterated food on the black market rose. Diseased meat, horse-flesh, damaged tinned goods, impure butter and cheese, watered beer and whisky 30° under proof were frequently discovered by inspectors, but the problem was most serious with milk.

During the First World War an important source of supply was the one-man business. These were set up in small shops with a shed nearby housing six or seven cows. Competition between firms was intense, wages low, and roundsmen expected to make them up by fiddles. One of these 'was to knock up the bottom of the can (and with an easy-going customer the front of the can as well). In some cases the milkman might be able to "save" a quarter of a pint in this way. "Chance" sales were an absolutely essential part of the milkman's existence.' They gave him an opportunity to sell the milk he had fiddled. 'With the big houses with weekly or monthly accounts there was collusion with the house-keeper, who would order a pound of butter and ask to be charged for two pounds.' In 1910 one milkman earned about £1 5s 0d a week and made another £1 5s 0d on fiddles. From 1910 to 1916, when this man went into the forces, he had 'only three days holiday . . . you could not go sick otherwise your book-keeping would be discovered.'[7]

Other dairy concerns bought milk from the farm. Water was often added. During the war there were twenty-four serious cases of adulterating milk and countless minor ones. Numerous offenders were never caught. 'Many times on a hot summer day the milk would curdle in the churns because of the movement of the cart. I used to strain it through a piece of rag, otherwise I would have to pay for the milk. No one worried about hygiene . . .'[7] Courts were a lottery. In 1917-18 eight people were jailed. Frank Hewell went inside for three months in April 1918. John Davies of Milford Haven whose churns 'contained water only' was also jailed for three months in April 1918. In November William Eaton, a dairyman's assistant in the City, was jailed for a month for watering milk. A few weeks later a farmer named Hedges from Leighton Buzzard was prosecuted by Hackney Council. Churns belonging to him contained 50 per cent and 75 per cent water. The Council described this as one of the 'most awful' cases they had come across. He was fined £40.[8] Two months later he was back in court charged with a similar offence; this time the fine was £20. On the same day Thomas Hughes of Hackney was fined £5 for selling milk from which over 40 per cent of the fat had been abstracted.[9] Similar charges were brought before the London courts every few days.

Then, in the summer of 1919, milk dealers found a loop-hole in the law. They claimed they had a warranty from the supplier guaranteeing the quality of the milk and so could not be held responsible for any adulteration that had taken place. Magistrates were obliged to dismiss charges. The onus was now on the prosecutor to prove that the supplier had knowingly sold watered milk. But if he was able to produce a warranty from the farmer this charge failed too. Prosecuting farmers was not very fruitful either. They argued that the milk was in perfect condition when it left the farm. 'He knew there were thirsty railway porters,' one defendant explained. 'Milk was tampered with on the railway.' The magistrate was amused. 'That has only arisen, I suppose, since whisky became unobtainable.'[10]

Many dairies now felt they had carte blanche to add water to the milk they sold, while railway workers who *were* caught tampering with milk could expect rough treatment in the courts.[11] Councils continued to bring prosecutions hoping that bad publicity would act as a deterrent. But some firms like the Dairy Supply company of London were repeatedly prosecuted and repeatedly secured the dismissal of the charges. In September 1919 they gave a warranty for milk containing 24 per cent water. They argued that they had a 'reasonable belief' that the milk was pure and called as witnesses all the people who had handled it after it arrived in London. That left the farmer, but proceedings could not be taken against him because he had not supplied a guarantee. The magistrate dismissed the summons protesting that 'these prosecutions are absolutely farcical.'

Government attempts to supervise the food and drink market relaxed towards the end of 1919. The concluding episode was the profiteering act of that year.

The 'great age' of profiteering had been during the war itself when businessmen — those making munitions especially — 'shot up from nothing to great fortunes'.[12] The bills had been paid by the government; some workers had even benefitted as wages rose. But once the war was over and the government eased up on controls, prices shot up. They rose twice as fast in 1919 as during the worst years of the war and suddenly everyone knew a 'profiteer'. He was the corner shopkeeper who kept putting up the price of his goods. 'Profiteering' became a political issue. 'The profiteer has already been given far too much rope', declared one local newspaper in 1919. 'He has probably had more to do with the unrest and discontent that have prevailed in the country than all the Bolsheviks put together.'[13] The government bowed to pressure and introduced a profiteering bill which became law in October 1919. The act empowered local authorities to set up special committees which would hear allegations of

profiteering, hold inquiries and decide if the offender should
be prosecuted. Sir William Beveridge later described the act
as 'window-dressing . . . It made no appreciable difference
either to traders or to the course of prices.'[14] In fact it did
rather more than this. The Shoreditch profiteering committee
held twenty six meetings under the act to consider twenty one
complaints. They ordered six refunds, the amount being re-
paid totalling 2s 7½d. Sidney Brown and Co. of Hoxton sold
a box of chocolates to a customer for 10d which he discovered
he could have bought elsewhere for 9d. Brown admitted the
sale and the committee warned him not to do it again.[15]
Hackney profiteering committee heard three cases at its first
sitting. One was dismissed; refunds were ordered in the other
two. One came to 2½d.[16] The *Hackney Gazette* concluded
that when the shopkeeper contemplated the work of these
committees 'instead of going away and sinning no more he
would probably be tempted to embark on a systematic scheme
of extortion — if the only risk he ran was that of being sum-
moned occasionally before the Committee and being compelled to disgorge his ill-gotten gains in their particular cases.'[17]

Few cases were sent to court and those that did go produced
the usual variety of response from magistrates. 'A great deal
of the existing social unrest can be attributed to cases such as
this,' said a London stipendiary imposing a jail sentence on a
butcher who overcharged.[18] 'Profiteering is a serious offence,'
said another, 'in view of the present unrest.' But the chairman
of Stoke Newington Food Control Committee was dissatisfied
with the 'very inadequate fines and costs' passed at North
London court. These amounted to only half the expenses of
the committee. The whole business was 'a waste of time'.[19]
Shoreditch Committee's experience was also dispiriting. The
only case of profiteering they sent to court was dismissed because the item — a pot of cream — did not fall within the
act.[20]

The post-war boom broke in 1921. Wage rates which had
reached a peak in 1920 had declined sharply by 1922. *The
Economist* calculated that the working man had lost three-
quarters of his wartime wage increases by then; the plight of
those who had lost their jobs as well was even more grim.
Prices also fell: the index of retail food prices declined from

291 in November 1920 to 195 in December 1921 (July 1914 = 100).[21] Overcharging was no longer an option in these circumstances. As the depression deepened and unemployment rose, manufacturers and retailers experienced increasing difficulty in finding markets. Hence the profiteering act died 'unhonoured and unsung'[22] in May 1921 though some businessmen had been so alarmed by its implications that they persuaded chambers of commerce to do what they could 'to prevent the possibility of its re-enactment.'[23]

Overall there were fewer black market prosecutions in 1919 than in the previous year. In England the number fell from over 24,000 to less than 18,000, in Scotland from 1,909 to 1,744, and in Wales from 2,452 to 2,289. In money terms the level of the average fine did not alter much[24] but the rise in inflation meant that the real value of the average fine fell.

The growth in unemployment and the decline in wages might have been expected to cause a rise in pilfering — it may indeed have done so but there was no reflection of this in the number of prosecutions. If we compare 1917 with a year of prosperity (1919) and one of recession (1922) the following pattern emerges:

*Number of convictions for pilfering of persons
aged 18 and over*

	Barnsley	Birkenhead	Brighton	North London	Walsall
1917	0	32	18	37	8
1919	2	37	7	8	0
1922	2	10	3	8	2

In Birkenhead dockers continued to provide most of the arrests in the town: nineteen in 1919 and eight in 1922. In 1919 George Taylor tried to leave Wallasey docks with eleven packets of Lux concealed about his person. Not surprisingly police thought he looked 'bulky' and searched him. James Payne took shirts and butter; George Doyle a bottle of brandy; William McCready, a nightwatchman at the docks, took twenty-four bottles of brandy. Alcohol was taken more often than any other goods in 1919. No employer mentioned the amount of pilfering as the reason for taking action and only one did so in 1922. None asked the court to impose a harsh sentence.

The position was different in London docks. In early 1921 the Chamber of Shipping held an inquiry which claimed to show that 'the evil of pilferage' had reached 'serious proportions'. One company discovered that whereas before the war claims averaged 1.44d per ton of cargo handled, now the average was 26.91d per ton, a considerable rise even when inflation is taken into account. The Chamber made a number of recommendations that were to become familiar over the years: more efficient supervision was needed; every pilferer who was caught should be prosecuted; courts must impose sterner punishments.[25] They did not mention the low wages paid to dockers or the hardships of the casual labour system. They could not even rely on their own policemen. Five weeks after the report was published three policemen employed by the Port of London authority were stopped leaving the dock by two other constables who had noted their 'bulky appearance'. They had wrapped stolen towels under their clothing. Their homes were searched and more stolen property was found at two of them.[26]

Very few pilferers stole to supply the black economy. In Birkenhead only one man did so. He was an employee at Cammell's who persuaded apprentices to take brass to a shop in the town. The owner was charged with receiving. Cammell's were usually tough with pilferers but on this occasion the company spokesman told the court he 'regretted' what had happened. The defendant was 'a most skilled workman' (such people were in short supply in 1919). The bench took the point and fined both men.[27]

In the other three provincial towns none of the people convicted sold what they had taken, but in north London six did so. For six months Samuel Kirby, a carman, left milk in a garden for a roundsman to pick up. He said he did it 'owing to the high cost of living': he could not keep a wife and seven children on a wage of £1 10s 8d a week. The court was not impressed and jailed him for three months. Another carman sold metal to a dealer. His employer said he would give him 'a second chance' and the court fined him £5. Henry Carter sold wood (fined £5); Ernest Johnson umbrellas (six months — but he had a previous conviction); and George Johnson milk. Catherine Skipp stole Christmas crackers and her employer noticed them in a shop near his factory. He asked the police to investigate and they discovered that Catherine and her daughter had been selling them to the caretaker of the flats where they lived. She in turn sold them to two shop-keepers. Catherine was fined £5; her daughter was bound over.[28]

In 1922 three pilferers had been selling stolen goods. William Clark sold sugar and was caught when a representative of his firm followed his van: the shortages had been noticed (one month jail). Joseph Appleby left Berger's, a firm which claimed to have a constant problem of pilfering, with tins of varnish suspended from his neck by a piece of string. He sold the tins for 4s, their 'value' being 10s. He too was jailed for a month. An anonymous letter drew the attention of the police to Henry Broadway. He was arrested taking paper stolen from Waterlow and Sons to a paper merchant (fined £5).

Nor did the black economy exercise any influence on the pattern of 'large-scale' thefts in the provincial towns though it may have done so in north London in 1919. Money or goods worth £100 or more were stolen once in Barnsley (in 1919) and once in Birkenhead (in 1922). Arthur Skipp broke into a private home in Birkenhead and stole a silver tea service; in Barnsley 'speculation' obliged Frederick Millgate to embezzle £625 from the shop he managed. He confessed to his employer and was jailed for six months. There were no such thefts in Walsall in either year.

In Brighton there were three in 1919 and six in 1922. All but one took place at hotels or in private homes; the hotels in particular attracted the attention of people the police described as 'professional' thieves. In 1919 Margaret Laurie, a servant, stole furs and diamonds from her employer; William Reynolds broke a safe at the Grand Theatre and took £124 — when he had spent the money he gave himself up. Frank Bernstein, a South African soldier, burgled the home of a businessman and pawned the property in Brighton and London. All three had often been in trouble with the police. So had Mary MacDonald, a thirty-year-old lady's companion, though the police described her as 'one of the most expert hotel thieves in the country'. In seven thefts in various Brighton hotels she took over £3,500 worth of furs and jewellery. When her home was searched all the property was found: several of the thefts had taken place in the previous year.[29]

In north London in 1919 the picture is different to this. There most of the twenty-six high-value thefts were of consumer goods. Cloth worth a total of £8,000 was taken in seven of them, from shops, warehouses and vans. Eleven business premises were raided and among the goods taken were 1,000 pairs of ladies' shoes, twenty-four chests of tea, 100,000 cigarettes, thirty rolls of cloth, £3,300 worth of blouses and stockings, £1,000 worth of watches and a vanload of meat.

In 1922 seven of the twenty-two thefts occurred at private homes: in four cases servants were charged. Consumer goods were taken less often: cloth worth a total of £1,350 in four thefts, mirrors, tyres and electric equipment in the other three. The remaining fifteen thefts were of jewellery, furs and stamps and included the six largest by value. In 1919 there had been four jewellery thefts but none of furs.

In the capital as a whole the Commissioner of the Metropolitan Police noted a 'substantial' rise in house-breaking and burglary in 1919 and 1920, although the objects stolen were often 'trifling'. The trend continued in 1921 'notwithstanding the widespread unemployment' but in 1922 theft showed a 'particularly marked' decline, specially in cases of house burglary and shopbreaking. The 'growth' crime was fraud and the Commissioner singled out for special mention 'complicated long firm' frauds.[30]

The high levels of taxation during the First World War had encouraged many businessmen to consider how tax might be evaded. A recent study has described how the Vestey family (who owned among many other concerns Dewhurst's the butchers) managed to avoid paying their share of tax, or indeed, any tax at all.[31] In 1915 they decided to move control of their businesses out of Britain. They established an American company in which they had a controlling interest and signed an agreement giving it the use of all their considerable foreign assets. This in effect avoided British taxation but the company was now vulnerable to the depredations of the American tax authorities. The family also had huge investments in Argentina where there was no taxation so the American concern was placed under the control of an Argentinian company.

The Vesteys were not the only rich Britons to avoid tax by making use of American facilities. When William Vestey consulted a Chicago tax lawyer on the matter, the man told him 'you are the third Englishman I've had in here this week on the same business.'[32] The Vestey brothers did not return to England until the war was over and then they made no secret of what they had done. When William Vestey gave evidence before the Royal Commission on Income Tax in 1919 he made the situation plain. He told the commissioners he was domiciled in Buenos Aires. 'The present position of affairs suits me admirably. I am abroad; I pay nothing ...'[33] Not only was there not an outcry about this, within three years William Vestey had been made a peer.

Tax evaders caught and prosecuted in the towns in this study were small-fry compared to the Vesteys. The majority of them were businessmen who had failed to buy health and insurance stamps for their employees. If we compare 1932 at the trough of the recession, with 1937 when economic recovery was at its peak the number of offenders convicted varied as follows:

	Barnsley	Birkenhead	Brighton	North London	Walsall
1932	0	1	0	36	6
1937	2	4	3	44	0

All these people were owners of small businesses. Although the sums of money evaded were trivial the failure to buy stamps could be a serious matter for the employees who found themselves without insurance cover if the business closed down or they were ill. Jesse Harrison, a manufacturer of children's shoes in Homerton, failed to buy stamps for six workers. The arrears amounted to nearly £16. He pleaded 'bad trade' and said he had shut down his business 'for the time being'. Samuel Cohen, a builder of Mile End, employed men for short periods 'by the nature of his work', made deductions from their wages but did not buy the stamps. Nineteen people were affected in 1929 (fined £1), twenty in 1931 (fined £14) and two in 1932 (fined £20). Jaffe and Harris, cabinet makers of Hoxton, owing £8 15s 8d, pleaded 'want of capital and bad debts', whilst Walter Probyn, also a cabinet maker, owing over £22, spoke of 'slackness of business'.[34]

Court proceedings reveal something of the twilight world of the small business in the 1930s, especially in the ramshackle factories and sweatshops of north London. When two inspectors visited the workplace of a garment manufacturer they heard 'a scurrying upstairs' as he tried to hide some of the girls he employed.[35] Three workmen at a furniture manufacturer's in Dalston complained that stamps had not been fixed to their cards although deductions had been made from their wages so an inspector paid the firm a visit. He learned that the police had been there before him. The brothers who owned the firm claimed they had been burgled and the insurance cards (all fully paid-up) stolen. The police noted that on their way to steal the cards the burglars had walked past a considerable amount of equipment but had not taken any of it.[36]

Most of the offenders were clothing or furniture manufacturers, builders or shopkeepers.[37] In 1932 only three owed £20 or more but in 1937 twelve owed over £20 and two over £100. Several were repeatedly prosecuted. A ladies' mantle manufacturer of Islington was charged five times between 1933 and 1937. Work people paid £95 for stamps which had not been bought. The magistrate told the man he had 'robbed' his employees and fined him £15.[38] William Ryder, a Birkenhead garage proprietor, failed to buy stamps for a mechanic for four years. Asked why, he said 'he thought it was not serious'. But the mechanic was out of benefit and if he had died his wife would have lost her pension.[39] William Page, a house furnisher in Walsall, employed a man for twenty years but did not buy insurance stamps although he made the deductions from his wages. When the man fell ill he found there was no benefit for him. The court fined Page £4.[40]

Fines were light even when there was a suspicion of fraud or theft. Esther Kastin of Dalston stuck sixty-eight stamps that had been 'chemically washed' to remove the cancellation marks on the cards of eight girls she employed. She said she had bought the stamps from a man who had gone out of business and did not realise there was something wrong with

them. The magistrate fined her £5. Henry Mills, a cartage
contractor, fixed over 400 'bad' stamps to employees' cards.
He had 'very foolishly' bought them from a stranger who was
closing down his business (fined £25). Cancellation marks on
the stamps in the books of employees of Alfred Rouse, a
bottle manufacturer, had almost been cleaned away by 'some
chemical process'.[41] Identifying such stamps required the
time-consuming attention of experts. Prosecuting counsel
were instructed to point out to the court how prevalent these
offences were but the fines (Rouse was fined £12) were too
low to be much of a deterrent. In north London one defendant
in three had used 'bad' stamps and in 1937 one in four did so.

Other businessmen bought stamps from thieves or forgers.
In 1934 three Londoners were convicted of 'trafficking' in
stamps which had been chemically cleaned and re-gummed.
When police stopped them in the street and searched them
they found over 900, worth about £67. In the first six months
of that year there had been fifty-five robberies in which
1,500 stamped insurance cards had been stolen. Two years
previously many purchasers of stolen stamps were traced
when the address book of a dealer was found. According to
the police such 'dealers' persuaded gangs of youths to break
into offices to steal the cards. The existence of a 'ready market'
was the motive but the businessmen who bought the stamps
had invariably had accidental encounters with the 'agents' or
'dealers' who sold them. They met in billiard halls, pubs, at
boxing matches, coffee stalls, in tube trains and railway
stations and on one occasion in a public lavatory. 'My wife
bought the stamps from a man who knew a man who bought
them from people who had gone bankrupt,' said one; another
was sent the stamps through the post by a 'well-wisher'.[42]
No-one ever seems to have been visited at his workplace or
home. Magistrates sometimes expressed disbelief or derision
but the fines they imposed were usually small. Defendants
stressed that a large fine might be the final blow to their
business.

Victims in these cases were poor and defenceless; in long-
firm fraud they were other members of the business community. Fraud was the 'typical' crime of the 1920s and 1930s
according to a senior policeman at Scotland Yard.[43] In the

depressed business environment of the period many firms found it necessary to offer credit on easy terms to develop a market for their goods. Purchasers expected to be allowed up to six weeks credit. Rents of warehouses and garages were often nominal so companies with very little capital behind them did not find it difficult to secure premises. The process of registering a company did not place any difficulty in the way of the dishonest. Undischarged bankrupts and people with criminal records even managed to take over reputable concerns.

The classic form of the long-firm fraud has a long history and examples have been traced as far back as the sixteenth century. A number of people with some capital would set up a business and order goods from wholesalers. They paid for the first orders to establish credit. Then much larger supplies were requested. These were sold for cash and the business closed down: weeks often elapsed before the wholesalers became suspicious and informed the police. By that time the frauds had disappeared.

In the 1920s and 1930s some long-firm frauds were more complex than this. Swindlers with sufficient resources would set up three or four separate businesses, each with its own accounts and stationery. They would provide references for one another if questions were asked. If the participants had 'good characters' (that is, no previous convictions) they might not abscond after selling the goods they had ordered but would salt away the proceeds and declare themselves bankrupt, supporting their case with falsified books showing fictitious losses. After all, bankruptcy was an all-too-frequent conclusion to much genuine business endeavour during the interwar period.

I have traced details of thirteen long-firm frauds which took place between 1927 and 1938. In 1927 William Farrington and Louis de Saraudy, an Austrian, took a shop in the Borough Market. They advertised for food supplies, paying for initial small orders but not later large ones. Farrington had two previous convictions for receiving and according to the police was 'an associate of South London thieves and was looked upon as a dangerous receiver'. Three years later Isaac Waxman carried out a similar fraud. He had gone bankrupt for nearly £27,000 in 1927 but managed in his new business to order goods worth £30,000. These were sold and the money he received was paid to relatives so his estate could not fall into the hands of creditors. In 1934 David Myers carried out a long-firm fraud and obtained £900 worth of supplies. He had a 'good character' and his counsel claimed that he was a genuine businessman who had got into difficulties. The police ruined this story by stating that Myers had been 'associated for two or three years with people interested in long firm frauds.' No-one was called to testify on the point: the word of the police was apparently enough for the court.[44] Altogether twenty-eight people were convicted but they did not apparently represent all those involved. Prosecutors claimed they were 'small-fry' or 'pawns': the 'big men' often escaped.[45] The sums of money mentioned in charges varied from £200 to £30,000 though the full value of the frauds was said to be much larger. Charges were only brought where the prosecution thought there was a good chance of conviction.

Defendants were mostly men of 'mature' years: only three were under thirty, eleven were in their thirties and seven in their forties. Two were over sixty. About half were of continental or American extraction. Ten had criminal records. One man had seven previous convictions, one five and one four. Seven had been made bankrupt. Nevertheless they were able to set up fresh companies and order large consignments of goods without difficulty. Six were jailed for three years or more while another twelve were given at least a year. Only two were jailed for less than a year.

By no means all long-firm frauds were caught. Dorothy Scannell has given a vivid picture of a pair who moved into her locality in the 1950s and the impact they had on the other shopkeepers.

> Along the road from us was a tiny, old shop . . . the window full of oddments. Bootlaces, faded reels of cotton, washing-up mops and various bits and pieces such as one would see in an old rag shop. I went into the shop one day for a reel of cotton. The proprietress had the appearance of a fairground assistant . . . She had well-dressed, reddish hair, good features, a plumpish figure, but it was her eyes which held me. They were such watchful, wary eyes . . . I won-

dered how she would make a living with the rubbish she had for stock. Her name was Chloe.

Some time later a male companion appeared in Chloe's shop, a husband, it was presumed. He was an enormous fellow, unkempt in a way . . . He had a drawling, transatlantic accent and the walk I remembered from my wartime days, the swaying sort of glide of the American soldier from Texas . . . 'I bet he's a deserter from the U.S. or Canadian Army' . . . A year later, however, the advent of Chloe and Ed was no laughing matter to the rest of the shopkeepers in our vicinity. Chloe took over large premises opposite. Modern shop fitments arrived, refrigerators, equipment of the latest and best quality, and, with "free gifts for all", one Monday morning Chloe's Grocery and Provision store opened (with a frozen *meat* counter!). Sadly, we all realised Chloe and Ed had come to stay and for months her busy shop held sway . . . We could not possibly compete . . . Chloe sold at under cost price, which was a mystery to all . . . [Then one day Chloe and Ed disappeared. The shop] was closed and the windows and shelves somehow looked curiously empty. Then the excitement began. Chloe and Ed were missing. Tales were rife. They'd obtained a large loan from a trusting finance company. They owed money to all the big wholesalers . . . the gossip went on and on [but] Chloe and Ed returned no more to the district . . .[46]

The economic recession of the 1930s provided the opportunity for another type of fraud: the bogus employment agency. Many people were prepared to pay to find work. Others were willing to invest a capital sum in a concern in exchange for a job. Legitimate concerns were established to bring together the two sides, but there also developed a shadow economy.

In 1934 three brothers called White advertised employment in insurance companies. Applicants would make an investment and then be invited for interview. The brothers also claimed to be able to secure jobs for lorry drivers. One man paid £50 and was given a driving test in a lorry hired for the occasion. He 'passed' and was told to report for work next day. Also in 1934, Laurence Marsh and four friends set up Trade Competitions Ltd which promised investors 'positions' at good salaries. Victims paid £280 to secure a job which payed £500 a year and expenses. An Oxford undergraduate gave £100 as 'security' for a job as secretary. Marsh had previously been fined for embezzlement and one of his partners had been bound over for obtaining credit by fraud. In 1935 George Robinson and two other men advertised for partners in a 'business transfer agency'. Applicants paid £125 each to join. This venture did not proceed very far because Inspector Frank Thompson of Hendon Police College answered the advertisement and was given an interview at which he posed as a North country businessman with money to invest.[47]

Bogus milk agencies were a feature of the period. Henry Collins and Maurice Jarvis set up Meadow Farm Dairies (Lambeth) Ltd, and South London Dairies Ltd. 'Men described as "boosters" were turned on several districts, and after they had worked up rounds by selling milk 1½d under the combine price, the rounds were sold. Sour milk and milk made from powder was then supplied to the roundsmen by the two dairies, some of the powder being eight years old. Following complaints from customers, the takings on the rounds dwindled and the roundsmen lost all their money.' Jarvis and Collins had obtained over £25,000 in this way.[48] Both men had records. Collins had seven convictions for long-firm frauds and larceny while Jarvis had been had up on a variety of charges including horse-stealing, receiving and false pretences. Another 'very clever' milk swindle in north London was run by a man on credit which he obtained without having to disclose that he was an undischarged bankrupt.[49]

Other frauds offered courses with employment guaranteed at the end. In 1935 John Loraine took premises in Wardour Street, the heart of the British film industry, and advertised a course for novice film directors and producers. A number of people had paid fees of £60 before the police caught up with him.[50] Eustace Hargreaves opened 'The Royal College of Literature' and recruited 921 students who paid a fee of two guineas each to take the entrance examination. Work as book reviewers was promised, after they had paid a deposit. Leslie Spikesman and four others advertised a range of postal courses, from show-card writing to glove-making. They received over £20,000 in fees.[51]

In ten prosecutions between 1932 and 1939 twenty-seven men and two women were convicted. Two were jailed for eight years, six for three years or more and another fifteen for at least a year. The majority were aged between thirty and fifty; two were over fifty and five were in their twenties. Six had records, for embezzlement, long-firm fraud or share-pushing. In terms of the amounts of money involved and its impact on legitimate business activities, share-pushing was a particularly serious problem in the 1930s.

In 1930 John Firth and six others formed the Economic Finance Corporation to invest in industry. They took an address in the City of London and distributed a booklet 'Wealth Through the Ages'. Firth and his friends were 'prepared' to accept sums between £5 and £50 to go to the initial investment account of £5,000. In fact they received £74,000. Investors 'in due course' were paid a dividend but that came from fresh subscriptions. Firth did try to make money, but on the roulette tables at Monte Carlo. The rest was spent 'in riotous living' in the West End of London.[52]

In 1931 Ernest Harborow became a partner in an 'old-established and respected' firm of stockbrokers. Four years later he was declared a defaulter on the stock exchange. About the same time he began selling shares in the 'Universal Carburation Company' to clients of his firm, raising about £13,000 before he was arrested. Stanley Spiro and his associates took control of a 'respectable' business, Maclean and Henderson of New Broad Street, and wrote to its clients, suggesting they re-invest in fresh stocks. If they were interested he paid them a visit, keeping records of the transactions. About one client he wrote 'wealthy man. Nice to speak to. Puts whisky bottle on table. Likes to talk a lot. Been in India. Been a rubber planter. Feel sure you will get him.' And he did, to the extent of securities worth £17,000.[53] Edward Guylee and two friends established 'Amalgamated Electrical and Lighting Equipment Company' and 'United Electric and Gas Industries', names which resembled those of legitimate concerns. They sent out 750,000 circulars to people known to hold shares, backed them up with visits by 'a small army of canvassers' and raised at least £130,000. Wetnall, Jenkins and Co, another share-pushing firm, received nearly one million pounds before its directors were arrested. When the firm was wound up it had assets of £55; £300,000 had 'disappeared'. Even this was not the largest sum secured by a share-pusher. That achievement belongs to Jacob Factor and his associates whose Broad Street Press received £1,600,000 for shares which turned out to be worthless.[54]

These sums of money dwarfed those raised by long-firm and employment frauds, to say nothing of pilferers. Jacob Factor had been active between 1929 and 1930 yet Spiro and Guylee, using similar methods, were able to defraud investors of considerable sums seven years later. The Board of Trade eventually decided that something needed to be done and a departmental committee was set up to enquire into the problem. This reported in 1937. It drew attention to the growth during the previous decade in the number of people wanting to buy shares and to the increase in limited liability companies formed each year. Share-pushers took advantage of these developments. They spent money to present an impressive 'City' image, taking offices near the London stock exchange. Share-pushers themselves were well-dressed men of 'good appearance'. They bought lists of people known to invest in shares and then circularised them with tempting bargain offers. Clients were persuaded either to give money or valuable securities for the share-pusher's stock, or to speculate with the share-pusher, depositing cash as security for the 'margin'. The share-pusher appropriated this margin by showing paper losses on shares that had never been bought. To 'hook' clients sometimes the share-pusher would buy genuine stock at a loss to himself and send it uninvited to the investor. Considerable numbers of people were caught by these techniques: one witness who appeared before the committee estimated that the activities of share-pushers accounted for £5 million a year.[55]

I have traced eleven prosecutions for share-pushing — the earliest in 1927, the latest in 1938 — in which thirty-eight men were convicted. The Board of Trade report claimed that share-pushers were 'most often English-speaking aliens' but the people prosecuted in these eleven cases were mainly English. They included a baronet, a lieutenant-colonel, graduates of Cambridge and London universities, and several sons of 'highly-respectable people'. Only seven of them had been born abroad. Twelve had records, usually for financial offences, and seven had been make bankrupt, two of them twice. Among them was Henry Brownlow (66), a director of the Universal Carburation Company. 'Since 1922 numerous complaints, about him had been received in relation to people losing large sums of money. He had acted in concert with international confidence tricksters and card-sharpers. Twice he had been adjudicated bankrupt, the last time in 1930 for £10,130. He seemed to have been living at the expense of other people all the time. He called himself a professional backer of horses and said he had been a joint-editor of a racing paper.'[56] Lieutenant-Colonel Edmund Octavius Eaton (65) 'has been notorious for many years as a shady company promotor. In general, his methods were to buy up or promote small public companies, and, having issued a large part of their nominal capital to himself for a fictitious consideration, he unloaded the capital on the public by flooding the country with documents described as offers for sale of shares and debentures.' Eaton's notoriety did not apparently extend to the country. He was 'a recognised leader of society in the South of England, and a well-known figure in the hunting field.'[57] William Preston (61) was the son of a solicitor and had been educated at King's College, London. He had spent nearly twenty years in jail for various offences: forgery (4 years' jail in 1894), forging title deeds (6 years' penal serviture in 1902), forging and uttering bankers' cheques (10 years' penal servitude in 1910). In 1930 he had offices near Chancery Lane and was a dealer in stocks and shares. He 'secured lists of investors in well-known and reliable companies, and circularised them to the effect that he had a client desirous of selling a block of shares in these companies at a favourable price. Replies arrived "in shoals".' He was spotted by a policeman in the street who recognised him as 'an old lag' and who followed him to his offices. When these were searched 3,000 letters were waiting to be posted off.[58]

Eight of the thirty-one share-pushers whose ages were recorded were sixty or over and another twelve were at least forty-five. Jail sentences were not notably harsher than those imposed on long-firm frauds. Twenty-six were jailed for less

than two years and five for as little as six months. These
included Gerald Corbett (36) who obtained nearly £12,000
through share-pushing (he was 'the son of highly respectable
people'),[59] and Sir Charles Buckworth Hearne-Soame (63).
Sir Percival Clarke, prosecuting, said 'the sympathy of every-
body must go out to a certain extent to him. He had fallen
on hard times. His income was small and his temptation to
join these companies very great.' He was apparently tempted
often. He had been made bankrupt twice and 'for the last
twenty years had allowed his title to be used as a sort of bait
in connection with doubtful companies.' One of his co-
defendants was jailed for four years.[60]

The Board of Trade report suggested that share-pushers
were assisted in their activities by 'flaws' in police organisation.
The exact sum of money defrauded by them will never be
known because many victims never reported what had
happened. Businessmen in particular feared press publicity
and preferred to suffer their loss in anonymity.[61] But even
when complaints were made the City police — which was the
force most closely concerned — was slow to follow them up.[62]
The continued existence of this police force was in itself an
anomaly and share-pushers were adept at operating in the
interstices between its area of authority and that of the
Metropolitan police. The Board of Trade found that between
1910 and 1937, 177 firms were known or suspected to be
share-pushers. Only thirty-seven were prosecuted. The City
police themselves did not prosecute a single offender after
1926. In nine cases action was taken by private persons and
in seventeen by the Director of Public Prosecutions. Share-
pushing and the Board of Trade enquiry do not indeed find
any echo in the reports of the City police. To judge from
these, share-pushing did not exist while forgery cases and
'offences against the currency' barely reached double figures
in most years.[63] The most lively issue in the early 1930s
seems to have been the impact of 'Special Measures of
Economy' on police pay. This was cut in October 1931 and
again in 1932 and the reductions had only been partially
restored by 1935.[64] The Board of Trade hinted that corruption played a part in enabling share-pushers to operate without much fear of the law though it insisted that responsibility

lay with junior, not senior, officers.[65] Yet the decision to withdraw the City solicitor was not made by a junior officer while allegations in court by share-pushers[66] that City police took bribes were never systematically explored.

The Board of Trade had criticised the poor liaison between the two London police forces and the fact that they adopted different methods of investigation. It now proposed that a central bureau to collate information on share-pushing be established and located at New Scotland Yard, and it invited the City force to take more decisive action in future. Share-pushing had flourished relatively unchecked because the authorities had not been sufficiently concerned to launch a thoroughgoing attack on it. There may have been a feeling on their part that those who invested in share-pushers' 'bargain offers' (so remarkable that any honest man would have thought twice about them) deserved all they got. Police as well as confidence men knew the underworld maxim: 'You can't con an honest man.'[67] But in the early 1930s some share-pushers were so successful that they threatened to divert funds away from genuine investments at a time when industry was particularly short of fresh capital. Share-pushing was sufficiently public an activity to make policing comparatively easy once the will and determination were there. Within a few years it had ceased to be a serious problem. Regular police work and tighter scrutiny by the stock exchange played their part but equally important was greater public awareness of the risks involved in speculation.

It was nonetheless disturbing that for a brief period more pilferers were prosecuted in a single year in London than share-pushers in twenty, despite the overwhelming disparity in the sums of money the two sorts of crime involved. In north London alone there were twenty-six convictions for pilfering in 1928, thirty-one in 1932, thirty-one in 1934 and forty-seven in 1937. No particular pattern emerges in the type of good stolen but prosecutors gave the impression that there were more instances of 'team-pilfering' and contacts with receivers than there had been earlier. A young man working at a chemical goods factory was followed when he left by two Flying Squad officers. He led them to a friend who in turn took them to the home of William Riches, who had a cut-price stall in the Ridley Road market. Property stolen from the factory was found at Riches' home. The company claimed to have lost over £5,000 worth of goods. Two van drivers at the Broad Street goods station took goods to an East End furriers. The LMS claimed to have suffered losses of property worth £2,300 and the charges against the two men referred to £650 of them. Alfred Littlejohn took screws and metal handles worth £1 19s 0d; his employer said he took him to court because he had lost goods worth 'hundreds of pounds'. Frances Kennedy stole eggs worth 1s 6d but the magistrate accepted that an example must be given to the 9,000 employees at Aereated Bread and jailed her. Albert Ince helped himself to 1s worth of milk when railway policemen were watching 'as a result of a very serious complaint from a milk company'.[67] Yet such people remained a small minority of those convicted. Four sold stolen goods in 1928, four in 1932, eleven in 1934 and seven in 1937. Nor were all these in touch with 'organised' receivers. Several sold property 'round the streets' or 'in pubs or clubs'.[68] Thefts of more than £10 of property were unusual. There were only two in 1928, four in 1932, seven in 1934 and eight in 1937.

In the provincial towns prosecutions for pilfering almost ceased. If we compare 1932 and 1937 we find that in Barnsley there were one and five convictions. Horace Richardson, a warehouseman at Barnsley British Co-operative Society (to give it its full title) was the only defendant in 1932. He stole boots and shoes worth £36 and sold them to his neighbours and at a local pub. Someone informed the police about him and he went to jail for six months. In 1937 four of the pilferers had stolen small quantities of metal; the fifth was Amelia Thurman who sold over forty dresses for one-fifth of their value. She was bound over, but her foster-mother was jailed for one month for receiving.[69]

Walsall had three convictions in 1932. A railwayman sold rugs valued at £8; the other defendants were Robert Roberts who pilfered a tape (value 7s 6d) and John Davies who took a necklace worth 2s 6d and sold it to a girl for 6d. According to his employer Davies was 'a rattling good workman' but he was not going to get his job back. He was put on probation for twelve months. Roberts on the other hand went to jail for six months. The police report described him as 'an inveterate liar, scamp, and out-and-out rotter'.[70] There were no cases at all in 1937.

Brighton had three convictions in both years, all trivial offences; Birkenhead four in 1932 and one in 1937. They included thefts of soda ash worth 4d, coal worth 3d, paint worth 7s 6d, tools worth 6s and a rope worth £2.

All four towns suffered serious unemployment in both years. In Birkenhead Cammell's had cut its labour force from over 6,000 in 1930 to less than 2,500 a year later. Nearly 6,000 men were still unemployed in the town in early 1937. Walsall suffered its 'worst year on record' in 1932 while Barnsley's coal industry was severely recessed throughout the 1930s. People who retained their jobs may not have cared to take any risks. Yet even in prosperous years Barnsley, Walsall and Brighton had very little *apparent* pilfering. Memoirs by contemporaries suggest that many people stole from their employers and were never caught. Nancy Sharman's uncle was a painter at Southampton docks. He 'kept the house well painted. He used to wear his Cunard coat to bring home paint from the docks. We had Cunard paint all over the house. Our kitchen was the colour of Cunard funnels . . . Clever Uncle Joe used to make rope mats for the house. He would plait long strands of rope and knit them on a huge frame or sew them in fancy patterns . . . Local people were quite willing to buy one of his hard-wearing mats.' The rope also came from the docks. 'I thought he looked extra fat — he was usually only a slight man . . . Mum helped him off with the coat and there, wound round his body, was a thick coil of hawser rope, stretching from his armpits to the top of his thighs . . .'[71]

Jan Jasper grew up in Hoxton, the son of a furniture deliverer. 'Of every three articles he delivered, one was nicked, and the proceeds shared among the men who loaded him up.' Most of Jan's family seem to have looked on pilfering as part of the job. His brother-in-law Gerry arranged 'a fiddle' at the fish and chip shop where he worked. Jan, aged nine, helped. His mother had been against this at first but was persuaded by the 'fiddled' fish and chips he brought home.

Jan's father's pilfering at the furniture business stopped when he was taken ill and another man took over. He discovered what had been going on and reported it to the boss. He 'let' Mr Jasper 'sweat' for a while and then told him he wouldn't be prosecuted because he had a wife and family. But he lost his job.[72]

Ron Barnes describes how his father 'thought for days' to find a way of fiddling his employer, a bookmaker. Eventually he found one but the bookmaker guessed what it was. None the less, 'the game' continued with Mr Barnes leaving longer intervals between each fiddle to calm the bookmaker's nerves — until he detected the next fiddle. 'There it is again. That little bleeder again. I wondered when he was due . . .' But Mr Barnes kept his job until the Second World War broke out.[73]

It sometimes seems that for nearly every job there was a fiddle. Some employers did not know what was going on, to judge from these accounts, others like the bookmaker were unable to 'prove' anything. Yet there may have been advantages for an employer in knowing that his employees pilfered, provided the overall amount did not rise above a certain level.[74] An unofficial wage in the form of thefts may have been cheaper than official wage increases negotiated by a trades union. The knowledge by both sides that employees pilfered also put them at a disadvantage in their dealings with employers. Some court cases may have been brought in order to re-establish the boundary of what was permitted and to warn employees what might happen if they stepped over it. Hence the almost apologetic remarks made by employers in certain cases, which so puzzled magistrates. Frederick Cattermole was a warehouseman at S. Simpson Ltd, a clothing manufacturer. This firm had a contract with a firm of rag dealers who would purchase cuttings. Cattermole 'worked out' additional sacks to the rag dealers and they paid him 'beer money' for this — about 5s a week (his wage was £3 5s 0d). The thefts had been going on for six months but Simpson's told the court 'having regard to his good record, the firm did not desire him to be punished by imprisonment or in any way seriously.'[75] Two workmen stole bedstead ends and a mattress but their employer was 'rather sympathetic' to them and reinstated them.[76] When six out of the fifty employees of a hardwood importer were discovered pilfering he offered two of them their jobs back.[77] Employers spoke up for six workpeople in 1928, five in 1932, seven in 1934 and five in 1937.

Magistrates in north London continued to jail pilferers: in 1934 over half of those convicted. In 1932 the proportion was one in five and in 1937 one in ten, though more pilferers were convicted in that year than in the earlier years. They fared much worse than the tax frauds. When Ivan Snell, magistrate at Old Street court, heard a case in which a businessman was charged with putting forged insurance stamps on his employees' cards, he fined him £5, even though he had told the tax inspectors three different stories about how he came by the stamps.[78] When William Redshaw, a goods porter charged with stealing a jumper worth 2s 6d, appeared before him he jailed him for two months. Redshaw insisted he found the jumper and had a 'good' character.[79] In 1928 and 1932 only one tax fraud was jailed (he had 'associated' with criminals); among those fined were several with 'bad' characters.[80]

4

The Black Economy and the
Second World War, 1939-45

When the Second World War broke out the authorities were
able to utilise the experience gained during the First World
War. They knew why black markets emerged and how they
functioned. Plans had already been made in anticipation of
an emergency and by the end of 1939 the organisational
structure of rationing and controls was ready. This was fortunate because the Second World War presented the British
government with greater and more prolonged economic
problems than had developed during the earlier war.

Three ministries controlled the market: Food; the Board
of Trade; and Supply. They were joined by the Ministry of
Fuel and Power in 1942. The minister most closely identified
by the public with food control was Lord Woolton, the
'human face' of rationing. He was appointed Minister of Food
by Neville Chamberlain in April 1940. Woolton provided a
strong lead and understood the importance of publicity in
consumer affairs. He used the media skilfully to put his
policies across and realised the need to anticipate events and
take advantage of them. He secured the support of public
opinion and kept it, an inestimable advantage. The lack of a
similar figure added to the Labour government's difficulties
after the war. The opponents of the coalition government
were never able to make a slogan like 'starve with Strachey
and shiver with Shinwell' stick against Woolton. Indeed the
war itself made the point about the necessity of food rationing while public opinion was receptive to the idea. Opinion
polls demonstrated considerable support for the system that
was introduced during 1940 and 1941.

The government intended to benefit from the experience
of the First World War in three main ways: rationing would

be simple to understand, egalitarian, and subject to strict legal controls. Woolton was determined that planned and systematic attempts at disruption would be severely punished. At the same time an ambiguity would emerge in the attitude of the authorities to the black market; not all its manifestations were vigorously suppressed. A certain level of black market trading seems to have been regarded as a useful safety valve, provided it did not grow too large. 'We could never had survived on rations during the war,' one contemporary remembers. 'The bit extra we bought on the black market kept us going.'

Food rationing was in full operation by the middle of 1942 and foodstuffs were divided into three main categories. Certain basic foods (bread, potatoes, fish, fresh vegetables) were not rationed at all but prices were strictly controlled and over-charging was illegal. A second group including fresh meat and fats was rationed and customers were obliged to shop with a particular retailer. Ration cards had to be cancelled and failure to do so was an offence. A third group of less essential foods (tinned meats, salmon, dried fruits, biscuits and so on) was governed by a points system which permitted the buyer to exercise a degree of choice. Rationing policy thus endeavoured to take individual tastes into account while introducing the principle of fair shares, but the overall quantities allowed to each person were spartan, to say the least. In 1943, for instance, each Briton was allowed per week somewhat less than a pound of meat, only eight ounces of sugar and four of bacon and ham. Some foods vanished from the shops altogether (mainly imports like bananas) while others were in extremely short supply and a rumour that, say, oranges were on sale at a certain shop would produce instant and often quarrelsome queues, especially if the supply ran out quickly.

The 'essential luxuries', beer and cigarettes, were not rationed but both were heavily taxed to soak up purchasing power and the price rose very considerably. Beer was greatly diluted and supplies arrived in the pubs eratically. The government intended that spirits should only be produced for export but occasional supplies from both licit and illicit stills did trickle through to the domestic market. As alcohol and tobacco were in such short supply, both became the object of much criminal activity: they were stolen, smuggled and illegally manufactured. This was also the position with cloth and clothing.

The Board of Trade supervised clothes rationing by the points system. Individuals were allocated so many points for a certain period and were allowed to choose among a range of items of clothing, each with a different points price. Here the purpose was to combine adequate provision for the community as a whole with the least possible diversion of manufacturing resources away from the war effort. The British received enough clothes to withstand the elements, while the poor were more adequately clothed (and fed) than they had ever been, but anyone who wanted more than his or her share would have to break the law, or face disappointment. Fortunately for them, the clothing manufacturing industry was particularly susceptible to black marketeering.

This industry still consisted of many small manufacturers operating from numerous tiny workshops in certain districts of the great cities and it had traditionally had an uneasy relationship with the law. Many entrepreneurs had sought to avoid the regulations governing hours and conditions of workers, and in the 1930s there had been particularly severe competition and price-cutting. Joe Jacobs has described succinctly what it was like to work in the clothing industry at that time: 'We were doubly exploited. The top worker was paid on a piece work basis and we were paid a daily rate or a percentage of the amount made in one week. The employer, who was usually an outworker for a manufacturer, was himself virtually a piece worker. So what happened was that the manufacturer would try to trick the master tailor, who in turn would try to trick his top workers who then did the same thing to the under-worker who was easy meat by virtue of his inexperience . . .'[1] Under wartime conditions of scarcity and the sudden sharp rise in the price of goods — provided one could find the materials and workers to manufacture them — this experience of 'trickery' could be turned to supplying the black market and outwitting the authorities. It is perhaps surprising that the rackets which developed in clothing were not very much more serious.

Clothing transactions between manufacturers and retailers had to be supported by the transfer of coupons, and the general importance of points in the retail economy made them a black market item in themselves. Coupons were illegally bought and sold, forged and stolen. Production runs were limited by law and one of the functions of the civil service inspectorate was to check that the law was obeyed. Manufacturers who exceeded their quota chanced prosecution and the penalties for this could be very heavy. The limitations the government imposed on consumer production were severe and excessive: they caused hardship during the war and exacerbated the difficulties of conversion to peacetime. It was the popular commitment to winning that kept the black market under control but even so, chronic shortages affected numerous essentials such as soap, washing powder, razor blades, toothpaste, combs and brushes. Trying to find a shop that sold them became an infuriating drudge of wartime life. Cosmetics, hair shampoos, and silk stockings were almost unobtainable. It hardly required a large productive effort to make them but the British government considered that even so small a saving of resources was worth the adverse impact on the morale of the population. It is a measure of their self-confidence: even Adolf Hitler had not dared to suppress the production of cosmetics.[2]

The manufacture of certain products such as jewellery, leather goods, glassware and toys was forbidden entirely and many Britons came to dread the approach of birthdays and Christmas. The second-hand supply of such items assumed increasing importance but the government followed the logic of controls and carefully regulated the second-hand market. Prices were monitored and offenders who overcharged prosecuted.

Rationing in the Second World War was more 'egalitarian' than in the First but the rich continued to be able to secure more than their 'fair share'. One loophole lay in the controls imposed on restaurants. A maximum price of 5s per meal was fixed and restrictions placed on the number of courses that could be served, but there was no limit to the number of meals a person might eat. If he had the means and the time there was nothing to stop him taking two lunches or dinners in separate restaurants. In fact one contemporary remembers seeing guests at a London restaurant complete one meal, walk out of the front door of the establishment, return immediately to a different table and order a second. For most of the population, however, the cost of eating out was prohibitive and they had to manage on their rations (unless they worked in a factory with its own canteen).

When the austerity of the middle and later stages of the war is recalled it can be seen that there were a number of dangers in the situation. The government had artificially created severe shortages of all luxuries and many necessities, and although the policy taken as a whole made a vital contribution to winning the war, the length of time it took to achieve victory meant that powerful unsatisfied demands built up. If there had been a seriously organised criminal community in the country this could well have been their opportunity. There is a parallel with the era of prohibition in the USA which enabled organised crime to create a position for itself in American life from which it has not since been dislodged. In Britain a wide range of products was vulnerable to the manipulation of organised crime: cigarettes, whisky, meat, cosmetics, coupons – the list is almost endless. But most criminals in the country at the start of the war were too disorganised and limited in their ambitions to take advantage of the possibilities; only those involved in the provision of illegal betting had the right kind of experience and they were broken at the start of the war. The aliens were imprisoned and horse-racing itself severely restricted. All the same, certain crimes such as large-scale theft showed growing evidence of organisation and sophistication during the later stages of the war. Fortunately countervailing forces kept them in check. Prohibition in the USA had not been reinforced by external circumstances: the country was at peace while its long borders with Canada and Mexico and its even longer coastline made it very vulnerable. Britain, on the other hand, was cut off from her neighbours by the war and public opinion supported both the war and rationing. There was no powerful minority determined, come-what-may, to flout the law, as there had been in the USA.

It is certain that if the wartime black market had shown

the potential for growth of the contemporary American and French black markets there would have been an outcry. Drastic action would have been taken. As it was, many members of the public furtively tried to buy 'just that little bit extra' to make 'life bearable' and many traders and business-men set out to satisfy them. The question for the historian to establish is the overall significance of the mass of 'little bits extra'. It seems that in aggregate they made much risk-taking and law-breaking worthwhile and justified the theft of many lorries and much breaking into warehouses and shops. Steal-ing, forging coupons, and illicit manufacturing was often attempted. But it is also certain that, as in the First World War, there was never 'a market'. No group of black marketeers controlled any commodity or interfered seriously with the supply of any product while the war lasted, although attempts to do so were made with at least two: poultry and coupons. Prompt action by the authorities defeated them.

This achievement is the greater when the increase in pur-chasing power during the war is taken into account. The mass unemployment of the interwar years had disappeared by the middle of 1941 and thereafter sharp labour shortages made themselves felt in many sectors of British industry. Trades union membership grew in line with this and although the unions did not make their bargaining power fully felt at this time, real earnings showed a substantial rise during a period when opportunities for expenditure were increasingly closed off. High taxes and forced saving (such as post-war credits) failed to absorb all the extra purchasing power with the result that too much money was chasing too few goods. Tradesmen and shopkeepers who overcharged could invariably find customers; the task the authorities set themselves was to ensure that sooner or later such black marketeers found them-selves overcharging a Ministry of Food or Board of Trade inspector.

If court activity is taken as a measure, serious black market offences were not committed in large numbers.[3] In north London in 1941 eleven persons were convicted; in 1942, twenty-one; in 1943, thirty-seven; in 1944, twenty; and in the first four months of 1945, five.

Overcharging was the commonest serious offence in 1941.

Seven persons were convicted and the goods involved were eggs (the subject of charges in five cases), onions and tinned food. Three of the defendants were wholesalers. Owen Brothers of Bethnal Green had been repeatedly warned for overcharging: they protested against the 'Gestapo-like methods' used to obtain evidence and were fined £50.[4] Two wholesalers were reported to the authorities by the retailers who bought from them. One was fined £100 and the other £120.

Three men were convicted of illicit dealing in timber. A man in Brick Lane sold £10,000 worth to 'unauthorised' dealers, people like Reuben Dell, a toy manufacturer in Bethnal Green. He made some £20,000 worth in the first quarter of 1941. The Board of Trade closed his business down.[5]

Two defendants were jailed (magistrates accused them of lying); the rest were fined. In 1942 four were jailed and five fined £500 or more. The commonest offence was still overcharging (twelve convictions). Defendants included eight directors of a poultry firm in Stepney: they overcharged retailers for some 50,000 fowls and were fined £5,250. C. Abbott of Bow supplied £12,000 worth of carpet fittings beyond their quota. The magistrate fined them only one-sixth of their illegal profits because he did not believe they had acted in 'bad faith'.[6] Sums mentioned in other cases were small. In only two did they go into four figures. Ingenious defences were sometimes offered. When Samuel Waterman, a poulterer of Stamford Hill, overcharged for poultry the customer complained to the Food Office. An inspector accompanied her next time she visited the shop. Waterman said he had charged the correct price and the customer failed to pick up all her change. He had actually been to her home to tell her this.[7]

In 1943 the biggest single category of offence was illegal manufacturing (fifteen convictions). The products were all in short supply in the middle of the war: furniture, bags, shoes, cosmetics and sweets. The quantities involved continued to be very small: 853 articles of furniture, £15,820 worth of bags, 2,000 cubic feet of timber. Buyers included Harrod's and Swan and Edgar. Six people were jailed for trafficking in stolen coupons (forgeries do not seem to have reached the market in 1943). Ten others were imprisoned, including four men who had diverted quantities of sugar allocated for honey and jam to the illegal manufacture of sweets. The prosecution talked of a 'network' of contacts in London and the south-east but only two sweet firms were prosecuted: one in North London and one in Slough.[8]

In 1944 the black market in clothing and illicit manufacturing accounted for eleven of the twenty convictions, and the black market in food for four. Clothing offences included selling stockings at nearly three times the official price (customers complained); overcharging and failing to take coupons (two Board of Trade inspectors were 'invited to enter the shop and buy the mackintosh without giving up coupons'); rubbing out utility marks on stockings and selling them at double the price. Illicit manufacturers made cycle baskets (250 dozen which sold for a total of £692 15s 0d), shopping bags, handbags and wallets; furniture and jewellery. Even in 1944 production runs were too small to have much effect on the economy. Albert Stokes of Walthamstow was allowed to manufacture £100 worth of goods a month but had in fact been producing up to three times that figure. When a Board of Trade accountant visited him he said he knew nothing about the restriction and produced his books which revealed what he had been doing. He was fined £395. Simon Fernley of Dalston made a profit of £461 on illegal sales of furniture. The prosecution said he had 'no books, no copy invoices, raw materials came from an illegal source and finally every obstruction was placed in the way of those whose duty it was to investigate the matter.' He was fined £850 and 150 guineas costs.[9]

Fines remained the preferred mode of punishment. Only one defendant was jailed in 1944, a poultry dealer who had falsified his books.

If the level of serious black market trading was low in north London it was even lower in the provincial towns. In Barnsley the courts did not consider that any offender had broken the law so seriously that a fine of £50 needed to be imposed. In Birkenhead the courts found five: one in 1941, one in 1943 and three in 1944. Many of Britain's imports from Ireland passed through the port but no organised 'fiddles' were discovered at the docks and the only 'smuggler' apprehended during the war was a Chinaman who tried to bring in a small number of silk stockings.[10]

Popular memory recounts the frequency of food and clothing 'rackets' around British and American military camps during the war. One was uncovered in Birkenhead but it did not amount to very much. Four RAF men altered a bacon slicer so the airmen at the base received even smaller portions and the surplus was sold to civilians, six of whom were prosecuted and fined £25 each; the RAF men went to jail.[11]

Walsall's numerous small saddlery, leather and metal businesses gave the town's economy a resemblance to the industrial structure of north London and similar possibilities for illicit manufacturing. Only three serious instances were discovered during the war: one each in 1941, 1943 and 1944. Leather goods manufacturers were limited to £100 worth of production a month unless they were working on government orders. Ernest Arrowsmith supplied £13,700 worth of goods in 1942 (mainly shopping bags) and the offences came to light as a result of routine enquiries by the Board of Trade. The prosecution said there was no question of a 'black market business' and accepted Arrowsmith's explanation that he had made the goods to keep his work people together and employed during an interval between government orders. The court fined him £2,100.[12] Quantities of goods mentioned in the other cases were even smaller.

There were eight prosecutions of retailers (several of them street traders) for routine black market offences. Walsall Food Control Committee kept a special watch on the town's market, so much so that inspectors became well known there even though they had increased in number from nine to sixty-four. In 1943 they paid 6,300 visits to retailers in the town, made 358 test purchases and initiated 114 prosecutions.[13] Only six resulted in fines of £50 or more and even there, according to the defendants, they had had to bend the evidence in their favour. One inspector was so 'well known and may I say admired that even in plain clothes people would know her', so was it likely anyone would try to sell her black market goods? Two other retailers denied self-incriminating words attributed to them but both had records and they were convicted. In another case, which went to appeal, the judge was so dissatisfied with the inspector's evidence that he quashed the fine which the lower court had imposed. He called the inspector 'a most unsatisfactory witness'.[14]

Brighton came closest to north London in terms of the number of serious offences. There were twenty-one convictions while the war lasted, the worst years being 1943 (seven) and 1944 (nine). People were convicted for the usual malpractices: overcharging, imposing a condition of sale, failing to take coupons. Representatives of some prominent landmarks in the town found themselves in court. The Norfolk Hotel was prosecuted in the Second World War as it had been in the First and for a similar offence, obtaining supplies of food beyond the permitted quantity (the bench took the view that there had been no attempt to 'deceive the authorities'). Other defendants were the leisure complex called the S.S. Brighton, the town's co-operative society and several of the department stores. Fines were very lenient. The Canadian Tyre company sold tyres when it was not allowed to; it also 'cooked the books' to disguise the offence and was fined £350. Among the purchasers was Hove Corporation (fined £25).[15] The co-operative society was found to have supplied coal to customers beyond the level permitted and moreover at a time of 'acute' local coal shortage. They had already been warned three times and the maximum fine was £20,000. But Brighton bench appreciated 'the difficulty of administering a business of this size' in wartime and fined the society £101.[16] Walsall magistrates fined a local coal company £1,400 for a very similar offence.[17] Brighton magistrates jailed no black market offender during the war, not even the shopkeeper and her daughter who chalked up fifteen convictions inside eighteen months.[18]

In Brighton as in Walsall allegations were made that inspectors were over-zealous. One shop assistant claimed that when she had asked a customer who was buying a coat for coupons, the customer replied she did not have any, 'took command of the situation', and wrote down for the assistant the price of the coat and coupons.[19] Defendants had to say something, of course, but in another case the prosecution admitted that the inspector invited the shopkeeper to sell a coat and not take coupons. She agreed and increased the price of the garment from £6 10s 0d to £7 17s 0d.[20]

It is impossible to know what proportion of retailers engaged in the black market during the war. Recollections of contemporaries suggest that many shoppers knew where black market goods could be obtained even if they themselves did not take advantage of their knowledge. Some customers refused to pay the overcharges such shopkeepers demanded or complained about attempts to impose a condition of sale. As food offices were reluctant to allow shoppers to change their retailers often, the protester could find himself at the mercy of the retailer. Complaints were 'paid back' in poor quality rations. A Wembley councillor observed in 1943 that 'cases had been brought to his notice of traders who had been prosecuted for breaches of the food regulations refusing to do business with people who had taken them to court'. He was concerned that this kind of 'blackmail' would stop other customers reporting black marketeers.[21] Customers who *paid* overcharges or accepted conditions of sale may thereby have placed themselves in a stronger position with the retailer. They were now in a position to 'blackmail' him into continuing to oblige them. Hence the need for an inspectorate to monitor what was happening 'without fear or favour'.

It is striking how often black marketeers who *were* taken to court had broken the law in a particularly flagrant manner. Morris Wohl, a Hackney shopkeeper, overcharged a customer buying sultanas and she reported him. The case resulted in his tenth conviction (the magistrate fined him and his wife £5 each).[22] A Wembley butcher accused of overcharging sought out the customer who had complained and offered her a 'handsome present' to change her evidence. She told the court, which fined him £20.[23] In north London in 1943 a man looking in a shop window was invited inside by the retailer. He sold him a coat, took no coupons, and gave him a receipt for £2 10s 0d (the coat had cost £6 17s 6d): 'If he was stopped by the police he was to show that.' The shopper was an inspector; enquiries he conducted revealed that no coupons had been paid into the firm's coupon banking account for some nine months.[24] The case was widely reported (two of the shop staff were jailed) yet a few months later in the same district of north London 'two Board of Trade inspectors . . . were invited' into a shop and sold clothes without being asked to give up coupons.[25] Similarly incautious approaches to customers and carelessly public behaviour, like carrying out black market transactions in pubs, happened frequently. A black marketeer who chose his customers with care, refused to deal with anyone who happened to walk into his shop, maintained good relations with business contacts (particularly with retailers if he was a wholesaler) and resisted the temptation to make a quick but risky profit would be unlucky to be caught. (Such a cautious man would not perhaps appear to be particularly well equipped for business success, let alone making money by breaking the law.) Once he had been convicted a black marketeer could expect to be watched closely. Inspectors would call to see if he was 'behaving himself'. Both sides were to some extent at the mercy of the records. Jack Miller, a north London butcher, had two convictions for overcharging. When he tried this a third time and the customer brought in the Food Office, Miller insisted that he had returned the correct change but 'a shilling had dropped on the counter and someone else had picked it up'. One of his customers indeed accompanied his wife to the Food Office to explain that she had been given a shilling too much in her change. Miller was jailed and when he appealed the sentence was increased to three months.[26] A year later in the same district a draper was fined £50 for a 'serious' coupon offence. His counsel insisted that this was an 'isolated' incident and the prosecution did not challenge him. Yet the same man had been fined £450 for a similar offence only a month earlier, but at a different London court.[27] This was the period of the V-bomb attacks and the efficiency of court records may have suffered as a result, but in Walsall, which was not affected by bombs, there was also occasional confusion about the previous history of offenders.[28]

Black market supplies in the Second World War came from three main sources: illicit manufacturing, theft and pilfering. If the amount of illicit manufacturing in these towns can be taken as a guide, it could not have contributed much to the black economy. There were nineteen convictions in North London, two in Walsall, one in Brighton and none at all in the other towns. The companies involved were usually tiny, often one-man businesses, and the quantities of goods and amounts of money mentioned in court were small. Only four had produced so much as £10,000 worth of goods; five had made less than £5,000 worth. Secrecy was essential in this type of production. The manufacturer would not want people to know what he was doing, certainly not his neighbours or business acquaintance. Securing labour and materials was an enormous problem. He would probably have to rely on retired people, while the materials would come from the black market. Hence illicit manufacturing tended to spring up in craft industries dominated by family firms. The most favourable conditions were found in business districts of cities which were deserted at night and quiet at weekends, like Covent Garden and parts of Stoke Newington. Goods were made for the 'legitimate' market during the day and for the black market in the evenings and at weekends.

Theft levels rose during the war. The trend may be exemplified by the figures for Leeds where £13,627 worth of property was stolen in 1938. By 1943 the figure had risen to £40,194 while in 1945 it reached £74,413, a rise of well over 400 per cent since 1938, much greater than the increase in inflation. [29] But these figures include all the property stolen; they do not indicate how much was taken in organised thefts. There is some evidence that the number of these rose in London during the war, but from a low base. [30] Most thefts remained 'miscellaneous simple larcenies'. [31]

Wartime shortages gave confidence tricksters an opportunity to exercise their skills. 'Whisky salesmen' offered bottles bearing famous labels for £5: inside was cold milkless tea. Others sold 'bathtub' gin which was alcohol but could also send the drinker temporarily blind. [32] More elaborately, a confidence-man might arrange with a forger to produce a document describing himself as an inspector at the Board of Trade. He dressed to look like a civil servant and visited businesses suspected of being involved in the black market. In north London 'large areas' were 'given over' to the black market in furniture. Cabinet makers placed their 'official' stock on the ground floor, but the upper rooms contained 'illegitimate stuff'. The 'inspector' would use his power of search to look for this material and would then allow himself to be bribed to say nothing about it.[33] These and similar ruses had little if any significant effect on the economy but press stories about them may well have influenced the public's perception of the seriousness of such crime during the war, making it seem much worse than it was.

Pilfering represented a third potential source for black market goods. If we compare the position in 1941, when wartime shortages were beginning to make themselves felt throughout the country, to 1944 when 'total war' was at its peak, and 1937, the most prosperous year of the 1930s, we find that there were fifty-seven convictions in 1937, 215 in 1941 and 186 in 1944.[34] The great majority of these were in Birkenhead and north London. Although prosecutions in the other towns were very infrequent, those that did take place had two things in common. Employers claimed they had a pilfering problem while employees had been trying to sell the goods they stole. A Barnsley glass worker stole a tumbler worth 2s 11½d; the firm had been losing 6,000 a week.[35] A trooper in the same town took army blankets and gave them to his wife. The War Office said they prosecuted the couple to obtain publicity rather than punishment.[36] A Walsall fire-watcher caught with stolen knives had also a 'typed reference and authority to sell goods, both of which he admitted he had prepared himself.'[37] Brighton post office trapped one of its employees by preparing a test parcel: he stole cigarettes from it. There had been 'a large number' of recent thefts.[38]

Most Birkenhead pilfering continued to take place in the docks and shipyards. People convicted for offences committed elsewhere in the town numbered eight in 1941 and nine in 1944. Dockyard security was stepped up in 1940 and 1941, the number of police on duty in the dock increased, patrols and searches were made more often. The obvious inference is that these changes were made in response to a rise in pilfering but this may not necessarily be so. The severity of the shipping crisis of 1941 alerted all levels of authority to the necessity of getting as high a proportion of goods through the port without loss as possible. Employers were no longer prepared to overlook small thefts. One docker protested when prosecuted for stealing meat: 'He did not think he was doing any harm. They had always had it from different masters in the past.'[39] But in 1941 more police were looking for pilfered goods and when they found them the man was taken to court. Two policemen were particularly energetic. Of twenty-one dockyard arrests reported in the Saturday editions of the *Birkenhead News* they accounted for fifteen. The bench congratulated them on their 'constant care and attention.'[40]

Cigarettes were the product taken most frequently in 1941 (eighteen cases), followed by clothing and shoes (fifteen), meat (eleven) and alcohol (five). The overwhelming majority of defendants had stolen for their own use: 'taking the goods home owing to the shortage', stealing 'cigarettes because he could not get any at the shops'.[41] Only one pilferer sold the goods he took (cigarettes which he sold in pubs) and no-one was prosecuted for receiving. Police had been asked by the National Dock Labour Corporation to pay special attention to this point. 'A strenuous effort should be made to identify and run to earth the receivers concerned which is one of the best methods of tackling the problem.'[42] That no receivers were found suggests that gain was not the motive of most dockyard pilferers in Birkenhead.

Thefts were small in value, the highest being £20 worth of sweets. Only five pilferers took goods worth more than £3.

By 1944 the number of police in the dock had been further strengthened (there were now eighty of them) and the chief constable of Birkenhead had introduced 'special measures'. These were not specified till a later report but apparently involved keeping a close watch on valuable cargoes. They had limited success according to the shipping companies. In 1943 losses through pilfering fell by 70 to 90 per cent but in 1944 the companies complained that 'a great deal of stealing continues.'[43] Police may have been able to stop most thefts of large articles but goods which were concealed about a man's person were much more difficult. In 1944 a labourer took £139 worth of cigarettes (four months jail), another £58 worth (one month); ten others stole property valued at £3 or more. At the other end of the scale, prosecutions of people who stole tiny quantities were rare in 1944: only one docker took less than 10s worth. In January 1941 alone seven dockers stole goods worth very little: they included meat (1s 3d), a sheep's head (6d), cigarettes (8s 6d) and rum (4s). Thefts of this type did not cease in 1944. The Ministry of Labour was seeking to coax workers to join the industry and promised applicants 'all the benefits' of the Docker's Charter.[44] These did not include pilfering but the authorities may have sought to avoid giving the impression that dockyards were 'nests of thieves.' They therefore preferred to warn in cases of trivial theft. No-one was prosecuted in 1944 for receiving pilfered goods.

In north London too there was a sharp rise in convictions compared to 1937. Prosecutions took place against a background of complaints from firms and businesses about the losses they were suffering. In 1941 Brown Brothers, a motor cycle manufacturer in Shoreditch lost £2,000; Ardath cigarettes, 100,000 in six months; Horne Brothers, £1,500 worth of clothing in nine months; £8,000 worth of surgical dressings went in a year and so on.[45] Company representatives certainly complained more often than they had in 1937 but wartime shortages meant they had more to lose. Production runs were now limited and every item that was produced could be sold. Firms called in the police more often and improved their own security. Press reports highlighted the activities of teams of pilferers and the deals they made with receivers. In January a motor driver, packer and warehouseman took goods to the home of one of them. From there they were sold to a local newsagent. The men pleaded the war in defence of what they'd done. One said 'his wife and child were evacuated and it was very difficult to keep two homes going'; another said he 'got into debt. We were bombed out and it seemed to upset me. I went off my balance or something.' The magistrate was not impressed and jailed them both. He seemed happier with the receiver who 'knew' the goods 'were cheap, so I had them. It is a job to get straight cigarettes.' He was fined £10.[46] In July a despatch clerk and a lorry driver were convicted of stealing bales of sanitary towels which they had sold for half their value. One of them was found to have savings of £200 and a bundle of war savings certificates. This was mentioned in evidence implying that they were bought with the proceeds of pilfering. It was presumably common knowledge that no working man could save such an amount out of his wages. The magistrate fined one of them £10 and put the other on probation.[47] The combination of a warehouseman or storekeeper and a van driver occurred particularly frequently in 1941. The substantial reduction in road traffic meant that it was possible for police to stop and search vans and lorries more often than they had in 1937.

Cloth and clothing, cigarettes and tobacco, food and alcohol were taken in about half the thefts though the quantities were usually small. Twenty-one people took goods worth £5 or more. Three thefts were valued at over £100. Despite the rise in convictions compared to 1937 only ten people had sold what they had stolen. Eleven persons were convicted of receiving, eight of them dealers or shopkeepers. Prices paid were usually about 40 to 50 per cent of the owner's value.

In 1944 goods stolen most often were the same as in 1941 with the addition of soap. Although substantial quantities were mentioned in some charges (100 combs, ten dozen bottles of hair shampoo, eleven dozen boxes of rouge, forty coats, sixty-nine bathroom mirrors, five cases of skimmed milk, 220 cases of corned beef, and so on) only eighteen people had sold pilfered goods while eleven were convicted of receiving. Six of them were retailers. Prices paid were very close to the owner's value, an indication of the scarcity of many items of food, clothing and household necessities at this stage of the war. The number of pilferers who stole goods worth £5 or more was twenty-eight, and four stole over £100 worth. Fifteen lorry drivers were taken to court in 1944 compared to twenty in 1941 and six in 1937.

A few people organised their pilfering like the packer at a tobacco factory who wore a specially constructed bag and the young woman who walked out of a hosiery factory wearing fifty-one items of underclothing. But such people were not very numerous. Most stole only as the occasion presented itself including some who took large quantities of goods. Robert Morris, a driver for Bouts-Tillotson, stopped the lorry he was driving and told his mate he would go and see what was in the load. He found clocks. Later he called at a cafe and took a clock in with him, offering it to a man he met there. 'It's no good to me,' he said. Morris could not take the carton he had broken open back to the depôt so he stopped and buried it in a hedge, covering it with leaves. Later he 'dug' it out and sold it for £5 to another lorry driver, giving his mate £2.[48]

Whether the amount of pilfering really increased or no, magistrates obtained the impression that it did from the rise in the number of prosecutions. In Birkenhead they responded by sending many of them to jail: 60 per cent in 1941 and 52 per cent in 1944.

In 1941 the proportion imprisoned rose during the course of the year as more people were arrested and brought to court. In January and February, eleven out of twenty-six convicted pilferers were jailed; in April, May and June, twelve out of fourteen. They included people with no previous convictions who had stolen whisky worth 4s 3d (one month), sugar worth 1s 9d (one month), silk stockings worth 6s 0d (fourteen days), shoes worth 10s 0d (three months). (It will be recalled that no black marketeering shopkeeper was jailed during the war by Birkenhead magistrates.)

The chief constable of Birkenhead said these tougher sentences contributed to the 'defeat' of the pilfering problem yet his own reports show that there were more thefts in 1942 (240) than in 1941 (206) while in 1943 there were 186 thefts and in 1944, 231. None the less dock workers continued to be jailed for trivial thefts.[49]

In north London magistrates jailed 15 per cent of offenders in 1941 and 20 per cent in 1944. More were fined: 36 per cent in 1941 and 56 per cent in 1944. Magistrates may have been influenced by comments made by employers. Some pointed out how serious a problem pilfering was and asked for appropriate sentences. A representative of Polikoff's, the clothing manufacturers, told the court hearing the case of a cutter who had taken cloth worth £2 10s 0d, 'thefts of cloth had been very prevalent since the rationing order came into force, and losses had amounted to several hundreds of pounds' (the man was fined £15) while a spokesman for Bovril said 'pilfering had increased to such an extent that it was felt that something must be done to set an example to the others.'

(The man had stolen two bottles of Bovril and was fined £5.)[50]

But these firms themselves were under pressure. Food, clothing and furniture manufacturers were now subject to accounting and controls by the Ministry of Food or the Board of Trade. Their reports and returns had to be available for scrutiny. Some black market prosecutions were based on them. A company which blamed pilferers for losses of goods might well feel obliged to prove the point in court. The police were invited to carry out special investigations. Six firms called them in during 1941 and four did so in 1944 (but none had in 1937).

Firms restricted to quota production could not afford any losses either. Clothing manufacturers could only obtain new stocks of cloth with coupons: cloth lost through pilfering would not of course produce any coupons in return. Everything had to be done to stop the thefts.[51] Only two arrests were made as a result of inquiries at work in 1937 but in 1941 there were twenty-two and in 1944, forty-three. Companies therefore were particularly alert to the possibility of pilfering during the war but although they prosecuted many employees they did not necessarily sack them. George Pickering, a general smith who had been employed by the same firm since he was fifteen (he was now fifty-eight), stole bars of copper and sold them to a general dealer. His employer asked the police to keep a watch on the factory and they arrested Pickering. Three hundred and seventy bars of copper worth £60 were mentioned in the charges yet the court was told that he would have his job back. The magistrate had presumably been considering a jail sentence. He said 'he was quite astonished when Pickering's employer said he would take him back. Stealing from an employer was a mean thing to do. He was in a position of trust . . . They were extremely good. He would not stand in Pickering's way' and bound him over for twelve months. The employer may have been extremely good and Pickering had after all spent his working life at the firm but the employer had also said 'his services were valuable and they could not replace him.'[52] Frederick Carle stole meat from the butcher he worked for. Presumably the thefts occurred regularly because they came to light when one of his children told a schoolteacher, 'Daddy has been bringing home meat in his Wellington boots.' Carle also got his job back.[53] A policeman saw Leslie Jones carrying a carton. It contained four vacuum flasks he had stolen from work. He had only been employed a year but did not lose his job. John Pope, a painter with three previous convictions, was carrying 14 lbs of stolen paint home when he was stopped by a policeman. His employer told the court that he did not wish to press the charge, adding 'if he had asked for the paint it would have been given to him.'[54] Altogether nineteen people kept their jobs (in 1937 five had done so). In 1944 twenty-six pilferers in north London retained their employment. They included people who had stolen clothes worth £40, coats valued at £120 (kept on 'partly because of staff difficulties and partly because she had given them good service'), mirrors worth £28, and tobacco worth £9. Emily Marrison was cautioned twice for stealing cigarettes from Wix and Sons; the third time the firm 'reluctantly' decided to prosecute. As in most of these cases, the magistrate was influenced by the attitude of the firm. He bound her over and told her that if she could not pay the costs (12 guineas) because of 'hardship' they would not be pursued.[55]

In the First World War, government direction had eventually brought order to the market and kept profiteering and rackets under control; in the Second World War, the government was prepared in advance and despite the long duration of the war and the concomitant hardships, its position was never seriously challenged. Although many individual black market transactions took place, a 'market' as such did not emerge in any commodity, and Britain fared well by comparison with most continental countries and the United States. In the latter the black market took on 'immense proportions' and 'engulfed' the country 'in a relatively short period of time'.[56] In Europe only Germany came near to matching the success of the British. In Belgium, the black market 'defeated all attempts to suppress it' while in the Netherlands the rationing system functioned successfully during the early part of the war but collapsed in the 'hunger winter' of 1944.[57] In France rationing was only partially effective, not surprisingly in view of the meagre energy value of the rations which at 1,200 calories were only half the average consumed in 1938. The French black market made up the difference, but only for those sections of the population who could afford to pay the price. French black market prices exceeded the official rate by a wide range: as little as two to three on beef, but as much as ten to thirty on coal. The prices of goods not subject to official regulations rose by a factor of eight.[58] In Britain it was rare for black market prices to rise more than 150 per cent above the official maximum. The most serious over-charges occurred on clothing, furniture, poultry, eggs and beef, but only 'luxury' and 'non-necessity' items suffered overcharges which matched even the lowest continental ones, such as silk stockings (2½ times the official price), watches (2½), and combs (4).

The occupation was responsible for most of the economic problems of the continental countries involved in the war. In Germany itself, however, rationing of foodstuffs and consumer goods had worked, and prices, wages, and rents remained stable as long as the Nazi regime endured.[59] The public generally complied with the regulations, motivated by patri-otism and support for the government, while the minority which was determined to black marketeer risked being handed over to the Gestapo for punishment if they were caught. Crimes against the economic legislation were punishable by death or sentence to a concentration camp, which probably meant much the same thing. This ultimate sanction may well have made the difference in Germany and it is a tribute to the success of British rationing policy, based on a genuine sense of shared national sacrifice, that the country was able to escape both the draconian measures of the Germans and the rampant black marketeering of the United States.

5

The Black Economy in the Period
of Austerity, 1945-50

If the British people supposed that the return to peace would
be accompanied by an end to the rigours of wartime they
were soon disillusioned. The government, the higher levels of
the political parties, and 'informed opinion' already knew
that Britain faced enormous problems in readjusting to peacetime circumstances; the mass of the people were to learn that
truth through the bitter experience of the following three
years. It was fortunate that the general election of 1945 produced so decisive a result. The Labour Party was reinforced
in its mood of determination and had enough parliamentary
support to take unpopular decisions without fearing defeat.
The Conservative Party was demoralised and required several
years to recover its nerve: in the meantime Labour did not
need to keep 'looking over its shoulder' to see what the
opposition was doing. Despite the dire predictions of the
country's enemies (and some of her erstwhile allies), Britain
had 'won the war' but this was a mixed blessing as far as the
mood of the people was concerned. Victory had generated
considerable national self-confidence: if Hitler could be
beaten why worry about the 'dollar gap' and the rest of the
country's economic problems? Many people were no longer
in the mood to make sacrifices — they were looking for the
rewards of victory — yet the economic situation offered no
rewards and demanded yet more sacrifices. The extent of the
Labour Party's victory in the election of 1945 gave it a
breathing space but the country's problems and the mood of
the people ensured that it could only be brief.

Britain had paid for the war by consuming her capital,
borrowing, and heavy taxation. She had abandoned her
position as a trading nation and the requirements of the war

machine and the direct damage caused by enemy action had disrupted her productive capacity. The country was in effect living on lend-lease, and it received a brutal reminder of how its situation had changed when the Americans abruptly ended this after the defeat of Japan. Britain urgently needed an American loan to replace lend-lease, otherwise the country's economy would collapse from lack of food, raw materials, and fuel. Imports in 1945 were more than double exports: Britain suffered an adverse trade gap of £654 million pounds in a year when exports amounted to only £399 millions. A lengthy period had to be financed in order to mount an export drive that would close the gap. Lord Keynes was sent to America to negotiate terms, but the Americans already felt that they had paid for Britain's war effort and the agreement Keynes signed might have been negotiated with a hostile neutral rather than a supposed ally.

It has been estimated that to survive Britain needed to raise her exports to something like 175 per cent above the pre-war level in the disrupted international economy dominated for both raw materials and finished products by the USA. The 'dollar gap' became a fact of everyday life: dollars had to be earned at all costs and as high a proportion of resources as could be managed devoted to exports. This could only be done by holding down domestic consumer demand which in turn meant retaining and indeed strengthening the wartime system of controls. It proved somewhat less onerous to restrict expenditure than incomes, but the danger of too much spending power chasing too few goods was an inflationary explosion. A White Paper of January 1947 showed that in the previous year the total amount of income available after tax was well over £7,000 million, yet the value of goods and services on offer was only about six thousand millions. To remove the difference would require further unpopular increases in what were already punitively high levels of taxation; the government opted for strict price and production controls which involved an obvious risk of greater black marketeering.

Rationing was more severe after the war than during it. Bread was rationed for the first time in 1946 while potatoes were rationed at the end of 1947. Both were bitter experiences for the British public, not quickly or easily forgotten. Expatriate Britons visiting the country, and foreigners, were eagerly canvassed about their views of the situation and their usually gloomy answers masochistically repeated in the press. 'I just can't understand how you exist on the rations,' said a former inhabitant of Walsall now living in Long Beach, California. 'In America people . . . probably throw away as much as we in England eat.'[1] Sudden shortages hit the shops. 'Smokers searching for cigarettes in Walsall this week found the shortage more acute than at any time since 1940', the *Walsall Observer* noted,[2] and a week later printed a photograph of a long queue of mostly well-dressed women. 'It is cigarettes, of course . . . Walsall is among the places referred to by the Secretary of the Birmingham and Midland Tobacconists' Association when he complained that girls who served alone in branch tobacco shops had been subjected to insults, abuse, and bullying from . . . disappointed customers.'

In Birkenhead about the same time 'workers have been coming into town half an hour early to queue for cigarettes. To a great extent they have been unlucky.'[3] George Orwell created the title for his last novel by transposing the third and fourth digits of 1948. Perhaps some sections of the book present as vivid a picture of the immediate past as of the future:

A tremendous shout of hundreds of voices — women's voices — had burst from a sidestreet a little way ahead. It was a great formidable cry of anger and despair, a deep, loud 'Oh-o-o-o-oh!' that went humming on like the reverberation of a bell. His heart had leapt. It's started! he had thought. A riot! The proles are breaking loose at last. When he had reached the spot it was to see a mob of two or three hundred women crowding round the stalls of a street market, with faces as tragic as though they had been the doomed passengers on a sinking ship . . . It appeared that one of the stalls had been selling tin saucepans. They were wretched, flimsy things, but cooking-pots of any kind were always difficult to get. Now the supply had unexpectedly given out. The successful women, bumped and jostled by the rest, were trying to make off with their saucepans while dozens of others clamoured round the stall, accusing the stall keeper of favouritism and of having more saucepans somewhere in reserve . . .[4]

By the summer of 1946 shortages were hitting the consumer hard. Some retailers were asking double the official price for meat, vegetables and fruit. Common household goods could command prices out of all proportion to the cost of manufacturing them. Combs were sold at three times the official price (2s 6d instead of 10d), hairnets, pins and needles at double. Clothiers added up to one-third on the prices of a garment if they sold it and did not take coupons. Larger items such as sets of dining room furniture sold for just under double the legal price. The police and the inspectorate continued to be fully stretched monitoring what was happening. The number of serious offences committed in these towns rose above the wartime level but the figures show that the authorities were never in danger of losing control. In north London there were ten convictions for serious offences in 1945, seventeen in 1946, forty-six in 1947 and forty-seven in 1948 (the wartime peak was thirty-seven cases in 1943). Thereafter a decline took place, to nineteen in 1949 and seven in 1950. The pattern of serious offences in the provincial towns was roughly the same as this: in Birkenhead and Brighton the peak year was also 1948.[5]

Most north London cases in 1945 and 1946 were small-scale black market offences: overcharging, failing to keep accurate records, selling couponless goods. Six defendants had bought supplies from sources they refused to name. Fruit and vegetables 'from somewhere in the country', meat from 'a stranger' ('You know how it is: chaps keep coming in and offering things, so I just bought them'),[6] eggs from 'somewhere' in East Anglia. When a Ministry of Food inspector visited Morris Summers' shop in the East End and asked for tomatoes, Summers told him he did not have any. The inspector searched the shop and found two baskets of tomatoes. 'When Summers was asked for an explanation he asked a boy in the shop where they had come from. The boy was a bit bewildered and said "there's a lot more out there." The rest of a large consignment was found in the back. Summers said he had been away from the shop and that the boy must have taken them in.'[7] Cases of this kind attracted press attention: such tradesmen were responsible for the worst overcharges. But they were not organised black markets and the fine (£95) reflected that. There were two cases in 1945-60. A furnishing company made an illegal profit of 100 per cent on sales of £37,378. Journalists present noted that on both days of the trial 'the public gallery was full to capacity, many of those present being connected with the furniture trade in North and East London.' The principal defendant had two black market convictions, including a fine of £600 in 1943 for dealing in clothing coupons. This time he was fined £6,000, an amount that left him with over half of his unlawful profit.[8]

In the second case a poulterer was jailed for six months. He and his 'agent' sold poultry thought to have been bought in Scotland to West End restaurants and clubs. Charges related to twenty-one tons of birds worth £4,500. The Criterion restaurant was among the buyers.[9] These prosecutions took place at a time when local politicians were paying close attention to the black market. In the East End the Communist Party took the lead. It had had some success in the municipal elections of 1946, had secured representatives on several councils and was the main opposition to Labour on Stepney council. Anti-black market committees were formed to monitor what was happening. One was established in Hackney in August 1946. The chairman was the Communist chairman of the Trades Council and the secretary an official of South Hackney Labour Party. Two Labour MPs and several clergy joined the committee which demanded tougher penalties for offenders and much greater use by the local authority of its power to withdrawn tradesmen's licences. Members collected a dossier on local tradesmen who had been accused of black marketeering, and this was eventually handed to the local food enforcement officer. They also uncovered some unpleasant practices among restauranteurs. Twelve of twenty-three cafés they visited were found to be serving horseflesh with other meat without warning their customers. The committee investigated the local wholesale markets and watched the traders there insisting on conditions of sale 'quite openly, as though they were regarded as quite the natural thing.' Edward Martell, a Liberal LCC member for Bethnal Green, confirmed the claim.[10]

While Hackney committee sought to bring pressure on the authorities from the outside, in Stepney the Food Control Committee itself took a leading role. Alderman Vogler, the chairman, lead a campaign against black marketeering and when an instance was discovered they prosecuted. He warned offenders that penalties would be 'heavy'.[11]

During these years, 1946 and 1947, the post-war economic difficulties were coming to a head. The fuel shortage paralysed many industries. Bread rationing in July 1946 symbolised for many of the public the misery of austerity. 'The war has been over twelve months,' one Birkenhead baker complained, 'and now we have come down to rationing the people's staple food.' A doctor warned that dock labourers and other heavy manual labourers were not getting 'enough' to eat. 'I don't think anyone could carry on were it not that the black market seems to be bigger than the legitimate market.'[12] The war was over, 'doing one's bit' to 'save the pound' was inevitably less effective as a slogan that doing it to defeat Hitler; shortages and the absence of luxuries had lasted a long time and the future offered no relief; the country's organised criminals were experienced in catering for the black market and had been reinforced, if the police were correct, by service personnel who were able to turn the skills they learned in the forces to the pursuit of crime. The situation could hardly have been more favourable for a mutual expansion of professional crime and the black market. Yet it cannot be said, on the basis of the experience of these towns, that the gloomiest predictions were realised.

The manifestations of black market trading as described in court included overcharges of 100 per cent and in a few cases the excess rose to 150 per cent (beef) and 200-270 per cent (eggs). Goods on sale had sometimes been obtained by theft. Loaded lorries were stolen and warehouses raided. In 1947-8 one defendant in ten in serious cases in north London had bought goods from a source they were unable to name (the implication being that they were stolen).

In 1947 an outfitter and his mother-in-law who owned a

stall in Stepney were 'raided' by police. They had a quantity of stockings but would not say where they had obtained them. The police had acted on information and argued the stockings were stolen but the magistrate dismissed this part of the charges.[13] Quantities of goods listed in all but one of the cases covered here were small: sixty pairs of socks, thirty-five tablets of soap, a single rabbit, six watches, eighty-one bottles of spirits, 130 pairs of nylons. Sentencing reflected this.[14] In 1947 and 1948 only four north London black marketeers were jailed, all for short terms (four months or less). And by 'black market' magistrates understood cases like the following: four street traders were discovered by police carving up pork in a garage. The 'man in charge', a fruiterer, would only say that a stranger driving a lorry had happened to stop at his stall and offer him the meat. Yet the police had known enough about the case to catch them in the act of dividing it up.[15] They found the carcases of four pigs. One street trader was jailed, the others were fined £60 each.

During 1946 and 1947 smuggled goods found their way into the shops. With the resumption of trade between Britain and the continent legitimate transactions were supposed to have been matched by many illegitimate ones. British and American military personnel were said to be heavily involved. Yet here too the quantities of goods discovered by police and customs officers were trivial. Only one smuggler on any kind of scale was prosecuted in the north London courts in 1946-8. He was a wholesale skin merchant who imported bales of rabbit skins from Belgium. These were stuffed with parcels of watches, 4,000 of them. He said he had paid £8,000 for them in Belgium, packing and posting them himself, but the court preferred to believe he was 'the agent' for a 'much bigger' organisation. He was fined £25,000.[16] The other prosecutions involved tiny quantities of goods, such as 17,400 cigarettes and 144 bracelets, sold by young watch repairers or jewellers. They insisted they bought them from 'strangers' who 'happened' to call in their shops or whom they 'encountered' in a pub or the street.[17]

Birkenhead also saw the arrest of a number of smugglers but these were even smaller fry than their equivalents in

London. A Belgian ship's steward tried to take 10,000 cigarettes through customs, was caught and fined £100. Four members of a Norwegian tanker crew tried to do the same and were fined £135. In 1945-9 twelve men were convicted, most of them foreign seamen. They had tried to smuggle cigarettes, nylons or watches. Only one purchaser was prosecuted. This was Mrs Fletcher, a tobacconist. A policeman noticed she was selling American cigarettes labelled ship's stores. She said she'd bought them from a 'friend' who had bought them from a seaman. She claimed she was making no money — they cost her almost as much as the price she paid. She wanted them to 'satisfy' her customers. The court fined her £5 19s 3d.[18]

Black marketeering in the provincial towns between 1945 and 1950 invariably involved overcharging, failing to take coupons, or buying or selling 'unauthorised' goods. Military and public canteens suffered occasional 'fiddles' on the part of their staff. There were two instances in Birkenhead. Naval petty officers at the NAAFI were fined for pilfering food in 1945.[19] Three years later, staff at a council cooking centre sold meat to retailers and caterers, including one who had been a member of Birkenhead Watch Committee for several years. Five canteen staff went to jail but the shopkeepers were fined £60 or £70.[20]

Courts in the provincial towns did not find any black market offence committed by a businessman sufficiently alarming to warrant jail. The highest fines were imposed in Barnsley in a case which was a small part of an attempt to create 'a market' in fruit and vegetables, the only instance of its kind in these towns during the 1940s. A London importer of fruit and vegetables, J. and J. Lyons, insisted that when customers in the wholesale trade bought pears or onions they pay a surcharge. In Barnsley the additions on substantial quantities of goods varied between 15 per cent and 40 per cent. The surcharge was of course illegal and the transactions were accompanied by cash payments. Documentation would show only the legal price. Nine out of ten wholesalers who put in orders agreed to pay the surcharge. This would be passed on to the retailer and through him to the customer. J. and J. Lyons were so successful — and the shortage of fruit and vegetables in 1946-7 was sufficiently great that they 'almost cornered the whole of the market in imported American pears'. Wholesalers called on them carrying sacks full of pound notes (the Lyons' insisted on payment in cash). The senior partner would put the bundles of money on a table and throw an overcoat over them. Fines of £30,000 were imposed, though *in absentia* in the case of the elder Mr Lyons who had fled to the USA.[21]

There is thus little in the court evidence to confirm the reputation of the 1940s as a period when the black market throve. It may be that courts sometimes failed to sentence as sternly as prosecutors wished. In October 1946 a multiple grocer who had deliberately overdrawn coupons to receive extra supplies (equal to a month's food for over 8,000 people) was fined £60.[22] The surplus was sold on the black market while checking the points in the pre-calculator age meant that some official had had to count nearly 200,000 of them. A Spitalfields fruit wholesaler with a turnover of £150,000 a year was fined £20 for systematically over-charging in 1947,[23] Geoffrey Raphael, a magistrate at Thames court, confronted by three 'spivs' who had carried out 'a black market transaction, and a very serious matter too' fined those involved £50 and £25.[24] The same magistrate, seeking to make 'an example' of a wholesaler who had falsified documents, fined him £200. He appealed and London Sessions reduced the fine to £75.[25] Judge Neville Faulks, who prosecuted in a number of black market cases in the 1940s, recalls that he appeared against 'a very well-known company indeed for conspiring with another to contravene some order or other . . . Fifteen hundred dishonest and illegal agreements had been entered into. The companies pleaded "Not Guilty" but were found guilty. The Judge [Parker] said, "This is a particularly bad case, disclosing conspiracy amounting to barefaced contravention of the order, and I take a serious view of it." Fine: £5,000 and £150 costs each. Peanuts! Even so it was a lot for those days and I said to . . . the Clerk to the Central Criminal Court, "I say, that was more than I had anticipated."

"Well, what can you expect; the poor fellow's been down here for four weeks, and this is the first conviction he's had." '[26]

The fact remains that the offenders had been caught and prosecuted, even if in Faulks' view the fines were so inadequate that 'crime paid'.[26] Court sanctions against black marketeers were reinforced by public hostility. Some people had the money to pay overcharges or buy couponless clothing but many did not and the Labour government and local authorities had to take their feelings into account. In December 1947 Barnsley market was 'invaded by London "spivs" ' who had been 'driven from their holes and corners in London by the manpower hunt, the closer attentions of the police, and income tax officials'. They were 'strapping young men dressed in gaily ribboned slouch hats; the loudest and latest Yankee ties (nude figures painted with luminous paint); fancy overcoats with padded shoulders, highly polished shoes'. They tried to sell toy balloons at 2s 6d, paper flowers at 5s 0d a bunch and so on, not very successfully. 'Angry' Barnsley housewives refused to buy, complaining instead about their husbands having to 'slave' at the coalface to keep young men like 'those' in idleness.[27]

A more ambitious attempt to profit from the shortages of the time was also defeated. A number of men bought quantities of gelatine, rented premises in the town and manufactured table jellies. These sold widely and food enforcement officers were soon in pursuit of the wrong-doers. They arrived at the front door of their establishment almost as the black marketeers were leaving at the back. They abandoned all their equipment and a ton of illegally acquired gelatine. Conspiracy charges were brought against the two men who were eventually caught. Both of them were jailed, for fifteen and eighteen months. One, a chemist, had been fined £1,000 in 1944 for a similar offence.[28]

In Brighton at this time advantage of a different, more sinister sort, seems to have been taken of the black market. At a meeting of the Brighton Food Control Committee on August 23, 1945 the chairman asked the press to leave, then commented on rumours circulating in the town that bribes had been offered by 'people' wanting licences to open restaurants. A 'small' sub-committee was set up to investigate but that was the only reference to it in the minutes.[29] Eighteen months later a senior councillor, Alderman Aldrich, raised the issue again. He claimed that 'bribery and corruption' among officials 'had become an absolute scandal . . . I could quote allegation after allegation.' He suggested that when applicants for licenses successfully appealed against decisions by the local food office they became 'the victims of persistent persecution'. The food office launched an investigation – not because they suspected an offence had been committed – but in the hope of discovering evidence that would provide the basis for a prosecution. In the event of a conviction the licence would be cancelled. The food office thereby destroyed competition against its 'friends'. Aldrich recounted how one un-named official had gone to the home of a caterer on the Monday before Easter and returned every day that week. 'He overhauled every piece of paper he could find in the office and the longer he went on the less he found and the more exasperated he became. He was finally ordered out and another official arrived the next day and said the caterer would be prosecuted for obstructing the official in the course of his duty.'[30]

The Mayor of Brighton was chairman of the Food Control Committee and he asked the Ministry of Food itself to intervene. In the event the ministry proved reluctant to do anything. Only when the committee threatened to resign 'en bloc' did it give way and set up an inquiry.[31] This began to hear evidence in August 1947 but did not report until the beginning of 1948. Aldrich had made three main allegations: that long delays occurred in granting catering licenses; that these licences then contained 'improper' restrictive conditions which were only removed on payment of bribes, 'in cash or in kind'; and that officials followed 'improper' procedures when investigating supposed offences. The difficulty was how to substantiate a claim that a bribe had been requested by an official when no other person but the applicant had been present.

The Ministry of Food was not impressed by the allegations. It found them 'inadequate and unconvincing'. 'There were no grounds for thinking that any of the existing senior staff had carried out their duties improperly or incompetently.' But the accusations had not been made against existing staff. They referred to five officials, three of whom had since resigned and quit the town. They included the Food Executive Officer.[32] Aldrich was told that he need not offer evidence about them. When the ministry announced that it would circulate only part of its report there was an outcry in Brighton council. In March 1948 the Labour group voted for the first time on this issue with the Conservatives. It demanded that the full report be published. A Labour councillor proposed that the town's Conservative MPs be asked to bring pressure on the minister of food, John Strachey.

When the minister continued to resist, Brighton council sent a deputation to see him. It seems that a display of ministerial verbal skills persuaded the delegation there was nothing to worry about while they were with him, but when they returned to Brighton they realised they had gained nothing. The crucial parts of the report would not be revealed. To do so, Strachey said in a letter he wrote to the council, would 'impair the relations between a minister and his staff and discourage the making of full and frank reports to him in the future.' He added an attack on Alderman Aldrich ('sweeping allegations . . . unsupported charges of bribery') before admitting that three of them were justified. There was a 'non-proven' verdict in others. No-one would be prosecuted.[33]

This was in effect the end of the matter. Rumblings continued for some time in Brighton council and the local press but in October 1948 the council voted to 'receive' but not 'accept' the letter.[34] They added a resolution of 'complete confidence' in Aldrich and other people criticised in the report.

A storm in a teacup perhaps, but the minister of food presumably did not think so. His decision to keep the matter as secret as possible may have been related to growing disquiet in government circles about the activities of some junior ministers. These eventually caused so much concern that the Lynskey Tribunal was set up to enquire into them. The key figure, who attracted most of the press attention, was Sydney Stanley (real name Solomon Koszycki), a 'contact man'. Stanley's early business career had not been a success and ended in bankruptcy. In 1933 he had been served with a deportation order (he had been born in Eastern Europe) but had somehow managed to evade it. By the 1940s he was making a living by claiming to be able to fix up deals that would circumvent the system of economic controls. He certainly had friends in appropriate government quarters: John Belcher, parliamentary secretary to the President of the Board of Trade, and Charles Key, Minister of Works. Both accepted gifts from Stanley who was sufficiently close to Belcher to telephone him every day.

One frequent topic was the problem of Sherman's Pools, whose owner was another acquaintance of Stanley's. Sherman was dissatisfied with the allocation of paper made to his firm by the Football Pool Promoter's Association, the controlling body. The other pool companies retaliated by making allegations about Sherman's business methods which led the Board of Trade to open proceedings against him in January 1948. Stanley contrived a meeting between Belcher and Sherman; within eight days the proceedings were dropped. Sherman was not content. He wanted an increase in his paper allocation. When Belcher refused, Sherman accused him of taking bribes with Stanley as the intermediary. Belcher threatened to report the matter to the police but did not do so. They were in fact already interested in Stanley because of other questionable deals in which he had been involved. Rumours spread and a senior judge, Lynskey, was asked to preside over a tribunal of enquiry. Evidence was presented to it by the attorney-general, Sir Hartley Shawcross, a young and ambitious member of the government into whose alleged corruption the tribunal was enquiring.

The tribunal found that Belcher and a senior public official had taken bribes, though they were paltry — an occasional crate of alcohol, a gold cigarette case, a new suit. Stanley was the star witness and played to his audience (asked by Shawcross for his version of the truth he replied 'do not try to trap me with the truth'). He flung accusations about, claimed to have had 'dealings' with Ernest Bevin, Morgan Phillips, Sir Frank Soskice. Stanley's almost unbalanced garrulity may have served to disarm informed criticism: he was too comic a figure to take seriously. The Lynskey tribunal found only very limited evidence of corruption in the government. John Belcher resigned his office and gave up his seat in parliament. Both houses voted to accept the report.[35] The matter was closed. It now appears, however, that corruption in the Labour government was more widespread than was realised even by informed opinion at the time. In May 1974 Lord Shawcross wrote to *The Times* to say that when he was president of the Board of Trade (1951) 'knowledge' came to him about 'one individual occupying a far more exalted position than the comparatively small fry concerned in recent cases' and caused him 'a good deal of anxiety', while shortly after he heard 'incontrovertible evidence' of corruption involving large sums on the part of another 'individual highly placed in public life'.[36] He did not do anything about either and even in 1974 did not name names. The 'small fry' he referred to were John Poulson and his associates and recent studies of that case[37] have shown that it was during the period 1945-50 that the Pontefract-based architect made key corrupt contacts in local government, the civil service and the nationalised industries. Among them was J.G. Hardy, a senior official at the Ministry of Works, who directed contracts to Poulson's business. Another contact at the Board of Trade granted industrial development certificates at a time when these were extremely difficult to obtain. He was rewarded, like Belcher, with bottles of scotch.

The British public in the late 1940s knew of this only what was said at the Lynskey tribunal but within a few months of the publication of the report a murder case involving another Stanley was in the headlines; it may be that the similarity between the names caused confusion in the public mind about a connection between the two and made the ramifications of the black market seem more serious than they were.

In January 1950 the trial of Brian Donald Hume for the murder of Stanley Setty opened in London. The circumstances of the attempt by Hume to dispose of the body by dropping parts of it out of an aeroplane caught the attention of the press, but revelations about the involvement of the two men in the black market helped to sustain public interest.

Stanley Setty's real name was Sulman Seti and he had been born in Baghdad in 1903. At the age of four he was brought to England by his parents. He entered business early, at sixteen, and his efforts were disastrous, ending eight years later with a jail sentence of eighteen months for numerous offences against the bankruptcy acts. During the 1930s he snatched a meagre living but the war was his opportunity. By 1947 he was established in the Euston area as a dealer in second-hand cars but this was a front for smuggling and deals in stolen petrol coupons. Setty also functioned as a kerbside banker, cashing cheques for people who wanted to cover up illegal transactions. It was also a dangerous occupation because it meant carrying large quantities of cash. Setty, however, was well-built and presumably thought that he could take care of himself.

At some point in 1945-6 Setty made the acquaintance of Donald Hume, a former RAF pilot who had also done well out of the war. Invalided out of the airforce, he had started his own radio and electrical shop. He designed and manufactured the 'Little Atom' toaster and sold 50,000 of them. An electrical towel rail and mechanical toys also did well. He secured labour by persuading men working for other firms to go sick — Hume paid them double time. He solved the problem of transport by paying lorry drivers to carry his goods as well as those of their employers. Perhaps he would have laid the foundations for a post-war business empire but Hume had other interests. He could not resist 'a tickle' and joined in lorry thefts. He also had a taste for high living but found that nights spent in Soho clubs could not be combined with days in the workshop. His business declined and by 1946-7 he had turned to deals in stolen cars and selling forged petrol coupons. He turned his experience as a pilot to use as a smuggler. As he himself described it, he became 'a super-spiv . . . on the creep for a shady deal'.

In October 1949 Setty disappeared; a few weeks later his body was found in the Essex marshes. Brilliant detective work identified him. Within a week Hume had been charged with his murder. He insisted that the attempt to dispose of Setty was one of his 'shady' deals. Three black market characters known as Max, Greenie and The Boy persuaded him to take parcels containing Setty's body on the understanding that they were bundles of plates used to forge petrol coupons. The story seems fantastic now but at the time it impressed enough of the jury to prevent them agreeing on the charge of murder. Hume was found guilty of being an accessory and was jailed for twelve years. Released, he sold his confession to a Sunday paper but the prosecuting counsel in the case, Christmas Humphreys, dismissed it, adding 'the truth, I believe, is uglier still.'[38]

During 1949-50 the government enjoyed growing success in its management of the economy. Bread came 'off points' in July 1948 and by the end of 1950 rationing had been abolished on clothing, furniture, petrol and soap, though it was retained on most staple foods and coal. Improved production reduced shortages though shopkeepers could still ask and obtain overcharges of 100 per cent and more. Courts were noticeably more lenient with offenders than they had been earlier. They found no serious offences in Birkenhead and only one in Barnsley. A farmer converted part of his buildings into a secret slaughterhouse. 'A secret door . . . which nine out of ten people would never have noticed' led to it. Cattle slaughtered there would have been sold at excess prices on the black market but the court fined him only £120.[39]

In Walsall courts heard three serious cases in 1949 and two in 1950, most of them overcharging by coal merchants. One defendant appeared twice. In early 1949 a butcher was fined for buying meat from a lorry driver. He explained that he had heard two men in a pub discussing meat they had for sale. They offered it to him and after some hesitation he bought it. 'He had never seen either of the drivers before and had no idea where the meat came from.' He said he 'had yielded to the temptation' because of the 'thought of old age pensioners "scratching" about for food'. He was fined £30.

Four months later he was back in court, charged with buying coal from a lorry driver who gave evidence against him. This time the court jailed him for three months but an appeal secured the substitution of a fine of £120. The lorry driver who pilfered the coal had been jailed and he stayed in jail.[40]

In Brighton there were ten serious cases in 1949-50 but only one involved a 'large' quantity of goods. Two men bought pottery from manufacturers claiming they proposed to export it; in fact the pottery, worth £4,574, was sold on the home market. Both men were jailed.[41]

In north London smuggling or dealing in smuggled goods

formed the largest group of serious cases: seven out of sixteen in 1949 and four out of six in 1950. When police examined the accounts of a jeweller he could not account for nine watches. He admitted buying them in 'Cutler-street, sometimes from one man and sometimes from another', adding 'the shortage of rolled gold watches is a making criminals of us all.'[42] Smuggled goods arrived in the post. A merchant seaman sent food parcels to relatives when he was in America; they were told not to open them till he collected them. They contained 750 pairs of nylons. All but one of the remaining offences were on a similar scale: considerable ingenuity was often directed to securing tiny quantities of goods.[43]

When dealing with other types of black market offence courts in north London seem to have become impatient with the continued necessity for prosecutions. A 50 per cent overcharge by a wholesaler who had three previous convictions (including a £300 fine at the Central Criminal Court) resulted in a fine of £200 in January 1949. Associated Supplies, in court for the third time for overcharging rugs, was fined £70. The prosecution pointed out that the court could make an order to close the business down; the magistrate replied that the company should be given 'one last chance'.[44] A street trader in Petticoat Lane with several similar convictions was fined £20 for overcharging nearly 100 per cent for nylons. When a firm of clothing manufacturers pleaded guilty in March 1949 to substantial overproduction and admitted illegal profits of nearly £13,000 the prosecution argued that a similar amount had to be imposed as a penalty 'unless the Court found there were special circumstances.' The magistrate, Geoffrey Raphael, proceeded to do precisely that, commenting on the 'impossible' situation the company was in. 'He had considerable sympathy for traders who found themselves the victims of a system which while strictly controlling profits, took no heed or interest in losses.'[45] Officials at the Ministry of Food and the Board of Trade did not become disheartened by the failure of courts to impose the penalties the law required. Considerable painstaking work went into establishing evidence for prosecutions during these years. Western Farm Products of Devon were detected in a very skilful method of overcharging. They included in the invoices items (such as a consignment of pigeons priced at £1,605) which were never sent and which were there to conceal the overcharges. A fur dealer who smuggled cultured pearls was trapped when inspectors managed to translate the 'peculiar Hebrew script' in which he kept his records.[46]

Successful black marketeers would presumably have a problem concealing their ill-gotten gains. Any transaction involving records — bank deposits, purchasing property — could be traced; claims to have won the money gambling would have been laughed out of court. Criminals' memoirs contain a number of anecdotes built round this difficulty. Billy Hill describes how he heard that a textile manufacturer kept 'the fortune' he made on the black market in his safe at home. So he 'trained' two of 'his men' to impersonate customs officers, armed them with a forged search warrant and sent them to the textile manufacturer's home. While they 'questioned' him and his family Hill 'raided' the safe. He took £65,000 but the textile manufacturer told the police he had lost £2,500.[47]

The profits of legitimate business activity also faced a threat — from the taxman. The tax burden of the war in its later stages was estimated at only 13 per cent to 17 per cent on wage-earners but 35 per cent to 44 per cent on non-wage earners. Wage incomes at constant 1947 prices and after taxation rose by 18 per cent between 1938 and 1947 while incomes from property fell by 15 per cent and salaries by 21 per cent. Not surprisingly, the decade was thought to be 'rich in tax evasion schemes, both for owners of shares and for top salaried persons in private industry and commerce. Various estimates exist for the understatement of these incomes in official statistics, but though it is known that it ran into hundreds of millions of pounds, in the nature of the case no reliable statements can be made.'[48] Peter Calvocoressi wonders why 'in the daunting economic stringency of the postwar decade, priority was not given to less costly but hardly less urgent reforms such as overhauling the tax system, which was not only a tangle but also a paradise for moneyed wide boys . . .'[49]

If Pollard and Calvocoressi are correct, considerable sums might have been recouped if tax evaders had been chased up and prosecuted. In these towns, however, prosecutions were very infrequent. None occurred in Barnsley or Walsall while the war continued while in Brighton there were only two. A manufacturing chemist's was fined £750 because its management had understated the amount of purchase tax that should have been paid by £3,000.[50] The second prosecution concerned a self-employed manufacturer of kettle cleaners made from sea-shells who was fined £500 for not declaring all his turnover and thereby avoiding purchase tax.[51]

Even in London the number of tax evaders convicted in the middle and late 1940s was tiny. If north, south and west London are considered[52] there were only eight convictions in 1943, ten in 1944, seven in 1945 and six in 1946. No company of any prominence was prosecuted. All the defendants had tried to avoid paying purchase tax, and a number had falsified their books or forged invoices to this end. The amount of tax involved was always small: £11,479 in the largest case, with only six others above £1,000. Two prosecutions were initiated for failing to pay £63 and £134. Defendants included three jewellers, three manufacturers of furniture, two of cosmetics, two of mirrors and two of clothing.

Sentences were lenient unless there was an element of fraud. Twenty-two defendants were fined, seventeen of them less than £150. The remainder were jailed but only two for more than three months. The general attitude of magistrates may be summed up by Daniel Hopkin's comment on a furniture manufacturer who had failed to register for purchase tax: 'This is a very bad case,' he said and fined the man £25.[53]

In the later 1940s prosecutions of tax evaders were even less frequent: only one each in Birkenhead and Brighton and none at all in Walsall and Barnsley. Ten prosecutions took place in north London between 1947 and 1950, involving manufacturers of leather goods, clothing, furniture, jewellery and cosmetics, two of whom were jailed and the rest fined, though only four more than £250. Offences were usually traced from correct returns filled in by their business contacts. It appears that 'top-salaried' tax evaders either did not exist or their evasion schemes were so skilfully organised that the inland revenue did not know about them or could not discover grounds for prosecution. Marginal businessmen would not be able to afford expensive advice from tax lawyers or accountants. A few of them turned for assistance to a different quarter. Myer Stone, a wholesale food distributor, had a 'very big' cash trade with small tradesmen and stall-keepers. The prosecution said he 'had done everything to impede the investigation . . . A robbery took place at his premises' which brought the inquiries to an end. The amount of tax he had evaded would never be known.[54] When a bag manufacturer was prosecuted for purchase-tax evasion and falsifying his records, evidence against him was based on books 'kept for his own private use' by his former manager. This man had been convicted of pilfering from the firm but the court was told that that offence occurred after inquiries had been opened into the question of tax evasion. The bag manufacturer produced a witness who claimed that the former manager had been selling pilfered bags in Petticoat Lane. This did not impede his own conviction. Two months later his witness ('a menace to society') was jailed for fraud.[55]

Prosecutions of employers who failed to buy health and insurance stamps almost ceased during the war: only one was reported in 1941 and one in 1944. J.F. Poynter, an electric lamp manufacturer, defrauded twenty employees of £180. He was fined £4 and two guineas costs.[56] There none the less continued to be a market in forged and stolen insurance stamps.[57]

Pilferers, on the other hand, continued to be arrested in large numbers in Birkenhead and north London. If we compare the number of convictions in 1947, when austerity was at its most harsh, to 1950, when economic conditions were slowly returning to 'normal', we find the following:

	Barnsley	Birkenhead	Brighton[58]	N. London	Walsall
1944	5	42	5	133	1
1947	8	20	3	109	4
1950	4	43	0	98	10

There were thus comparatively few convictions in Barnsley, Walsall and Brighton: the people involved mostly worked at a small number of factories. In Barnsley in 1947 seven of the eight were employed at Freeman and Co, a manufacturer of hot water bottles. Two men who had been selling the bottles were fined £4 each; the rest were bound over. All of them kept their jobs. In Walsall in the same year the four pilferers were employed at Oak Soles Ltd while in 1950 six of the ten worked at two firms in the town.

Dock theft remained the largest single category of pilfering in the post-war period in Birkenhead. *The Birkenhead News* commented on the 'unprecedented amount' which caused 'grave concern among dock officials, shipowners and the police'. It announced that 'a joint drive' had been 'mutually contrived'. Magistrates had issued 'stern' warnings.[59] The chief constable gave special attention to the problem. He argued that the 'technique' of dock theft was changing. 'In the past, whilst a fair number of occurrences came to my notice which indicated a tendency for dock worker gangs to make communal plunder of cargo, with individual share-outs of the proceeds, the latter was limited to the amount a man thought he could conceal about his person.' But now, dock theft had 'a new look' (this was 1948). 'The planning is done by background men, with ready markets for the quick disposal of bulk property. They have means of transport available and dock contacts to indicate valuable and suitable packages, to facilitate loading and exit.' He gave four examples of large thefts of cloth, listing 'background men' (a taxi driver, fried fish shop proprietor, a Liverpool tailor, a shipyard worker); 'contact men' (dock labourers); 'transport' (a lorry, a taxi cab), and where the property was 'disposed' (locally in every case). Goods taken in high value thefts in the provincial towns in this study were usually disposed of there. The thieves were rarely 'professional' and so did not have underworld contacts to help in selling them. Organised criminals from London did, however, carry out thefts in the provinces from the late 1940s onwards – by that time most of England seems to have become part of their 'manor'. In Walsall, for instance, there were four big thefts between 1945 and 1948. In the two largest £8,000 worth of goods, including nearly two million cigarettes, were stolen in raids on warehouses. Quantities of cloth stolen in the third turned up in a shop in Tottenham. In 1937, a typical pre-war year, no theft in Walsall (or in Barnsley or Birkenhead) involved goods worth so much as £150. In Birkenhead in 1948 alone there were twenty-eight thefts of goods worth at least £250. None the less, only four of these were carried out in the docks by dock labourers.

Security at the docks deteriorated sharply during the later stages of the war. The 'special' scheme of police surveillance had been abandoned in 1945 because of shortage of staff and was not reintroduced until 1947, while supervision at the docks and adjacent railway sidings was 'slack'. The supervisors at one dockside shed did not realise that cloth worth £1,366 had been stolen till it was recovered by the police. The chief constable complained that the watchmen were too often 'advanced in age', and 'physically unfitted' for the long hours of duty which were anyway not 'conducive' to 'regular and alert' supervision.[60] Finally, dock fencing had been damaged during the war and not replaced. People could trespass on dock property and there were not enough police to chase them away. His answer to the problem was to improve the pay of policemen so that the force would be able to compete with better-paid industry for recruits. Another answer was to stiffen sentencing. Those responsible for large-value thefts were sent to quarter sessions where punitive prison sentences were handed down. The dock labourer and lorry driver who stole the largest quantity of cloth in 1947 (£1,343 worth) were jailed for three years and fifteen months; the tailor and rag sorter who bought it went to jail for terms of four and three years. Prison sentences in similar cases varied between nine and twenty-one months. None the less, most dock thefts in 1947 as in earlier years were small in value. Men were prosecuted for taking coal worth 5d, salt cellars worth 5s, meat worth 4s. In 1944 fourteen pilferers took goods worth £3 or more; in 1947 eleven did so. Cloth and clothing were taken in ten thefts; wood and coal in four. A goods porter caught stealing 2s worth of timber said he 'took it for fuel', whilst a worker at Cammell's who stole a small quantity of coal said he had no fuel at home. The company complained in court it was losing a lot of coal (this was the winter of the fuel crisis); the local press headed reports of cases 'Coal Black Market Starts. Growing Trees Felled For Fuel.'[61] No-one was convicted of taking cigarettes in 1947 (there had been seven in 1944) and only one person of stealing meat (four in 1944). Seven people were convicted of receiving; two were tradesmen, the rest either relatives or friends of the pilferers.

Between 1947 and 1950 security at the docks was further tightened though the chief constable's proposal to introduce dog patrols was defeated by protests from the trades unions. In 1950 cigarettes and alcohol were stolen most often (in nineteen cases), cloth in ten and food in eight. Eighteen dock labourers and fifteen seamen were convicted. In 1947 only one seaman, a ship's cook, had been arrested: in 1950 police stepped up the frequency of searches at the docks. Few large-value thefts occurred. The biggest dock theft was a consignment of 30,000 cigarettes worth over £90; the next whisky worth £10. Only one man was sent to quarter sessions for sentence: he had taken £9 worth of cloth, had two previous convictions (both as a boy) and was fined £10. No-one was convicted of receiving.

In north London 109 pilferers were convicted in 1947 and ninety-eight in 1950 (there had been 133 in 1944). Press reports tended to stress the black market overtones of certain cases. A coat cutter, stopped by police in the street, was found to have cloth and canvas wrapped round his body. They went on to his home where 'a sewing machine was in use and it looked to the officer as if ladies' garments were being made up'. Ninety-one yards of material were 'recovered'. He was fined £20.[62] When the home of a paint mixer was searched seventy tins of paint were found. His employer, Ferguson Edwards, claimed in another prosecution that £160 worth of paint was being stolen from the factory each week. Sweets and soap were also taken frequently and occasionally in large quantities: pilferers were found to be carrying 137 slabs of chocolate, 152 tablets of soap, two pounds of fudge ('concealed under her skirt in a cloth bag tied round her waist'), 7,000 saccharine tablets, a dozen bottles of pastilles. Two policemen observed that Henry Moorby, a labourer at Bryant and May's, was of 'abnormal size' and could hardly walk so they took him into the police station and found that in the top of his trousers he had 'a sort of apron' containing 204 boxes of matches. Moorby had no record but he came up against a magistrate determined to 'do something' about pilfering. 'It is a shocking thing', Geoffrey Raphael said, 'to send people like you to prison but there is no other way of stopping it.'[63] Six weeks earlier Raphael made 'an example' of a wholesaler who systematically and repeatedly over-charged: he fined the man £200 (later reduced to £75 on appeal).[64] Moorby went to jail for four months.

These 'black market' pilfering cases were, however, a small minority. Only seven receivers were convicted in 1947 and six of these were friends or relatives of pilferers. Only one was a tradesman. Eighty of the 109 people convicted stole less than £3 worth of goods, many of them only a few shillings worth. An electrician carrying £15 worth of electrical equipment was arrested by police. The magistrate, Blake Odgers, asked why he wanted it. 'No special purpose, sir,' the man replied, 'I was just collecting it.' Odgers jailed him for six weeks. A stocking fitter who stole £5 worth of toys had seen 'others taking them, so I took some myself'. She was bound over. A porter who was a member of a cycling club in his spare time was asked if he could get some bicycle chains from work. He did and sold them to boys at the club. He was jailed for a month. Others gave what they had taken to friends and relatives. Several simply left the goods in their homes, to be found there by police when the worker was caught pilfering.

One north London pilferer in five was jailed in 1947, the same proportion as in 1944. The proportion in Birkenhead in 1947 was one in three. No employer there spoke up in court for a workman and only three did so in north London. In 1950 in both north London and Birkenhead two pilferers in five were jailed. Ten north London employers made favourable remarks about employees (none did so in Birken-head) with varying consequences for the offenders. When Daniel Hopkin, magistrate at North London court, heard that an employee had been sacked he often regarded that as 'punishment enough' and bound the defendant over. T.F. Davis at Old Street, on the other hand, took a lenient line with people who kept their jobs but punished more severely those who lost them.[65] Exceptions were rare though he some-times felt charitable towards offenders on Christmas Eve.[66]

In 1950, as in 1947, most pilferers (eighty-two out of

ninety-eight) stole less than £3 worth of goods. There was the usual minority of cases of organised pilfering: a carpenter at a sugar refinery left the works with eight bags of sugar tied to various parts of his body, five of them round his waist; a lorry driver sold parcels at a café on his route between London and the Midlands. Investigations were started when losses had mounted to £580 in four months. Another lorry driver working for a sub-contractor of Tate and Lyle gave sugar to his wife which she sold. The police came to hear of this and questioned her. The driver insisted the sugar was 'sweepings' from his lorry. Two labourers at a sweet factory overloaded a van with sugar which the driver sold to retailers. British Road Services seem to have had a particular problem with pilfering. During the year twenty employees of the recently nationalised concern were prosecuted, eleven of them as a result of police investigations at Goswell depot in Finsbury. One of the men told the police, 'I have only been there three weeks, and I had to muck in with the others or be pushed out.' Another said, 'this would never have happened if the others had not been doing the same thing' while a third remarked 'they are all at it. Either you are in with the rest or out of a job.' These explanations have the ring of truth but the magistrate (Sturge) was not impressed. He jailed all the men but one.[67] Two weeks later six employees of London and Provincial Bakeries were similarly caught and prosecuted. Only two men on the staff did not have pilfered goods on them when they were searched. The magistrate (Odgers) imposed small fines.[68]

In 1950 ten pilferers sold the goods they stole to receivers; seven relatives and friends and three shopkeepers were prosecuted. Another four people were proved to have sold what they had taken. Several pleaded poverty to explain what they had done. A BRS carman who had stolen two cartons of vests said his average wage was £5 10s 0d a week on which he had to support his wife and five children and also find £2 4s 0d rent for his LCC flat. The detective in charge of the case confirmed these facts but the magistrate (H.F.R. Sturge, salary in 1951 £2,000 per annum, about eight times that of the accused) still jailed the man for four months. 'Living beyond one's means could never be a ground or excuse for stealing', he said.[69]

Britain had survived the austerity of the immediate post-war period without a serious black market emerging. The drabness of these years, the shortages, the queueing, left a strong mark on the public memory but the spiv was never able to take advantage of them in the way that his French and Italian equivalents did. None the less, by 1949-50 public patience was nearly exhausted. The British had endured nearly a decade of austerity. The dismantling of controls did not begin a moment too soon. What might happen if controls were extended beyond public tolerance was demonstrated by the black market in petrol. The government had attempted to cut private motoring to the minimum to reduce petrol consumption and save dollars. From 1 June 1948 private motorists received a ration per month which would allow them to drive rather less than the return journey from London to Brighton. Business users were treated more generously and many of them sold their petrol to ordinary motorists. A committee was appointed to enquire into evasion of petrol rationing and estimated that black market consumption in 1947 amounted to 'rather more' than 10 per cent of total consumption by motor users.[70] The AA, RAC and Scottish RAC rejected this figure and argued the true one was over 30 per cent. This was despite the fact that two thousand people were employed to administer the controls. These were now strengthened. Commercial petrol was dyed pink and the range of spot checks on private motorists was increased. *The Times* wondered how the police could be expected to enforce a complicated set of regulations as well as keeping up there existing heavy responsibilities.[71] None the less offenders were apprehended and prosecuted though magistrates rarely imposed heavy fines.[72] But by October the new measures had demonstrated their effectiveness. Hugh Gaitskell, Minister of Fuel, announced that the black market in petrol had been defeated. He had estimated that it had been taking 100,000 tons but savings of well over double that amount were achieved.[73] Petrol rationing was finally brought to an end in May 1950.

6

The Black Economy in the Age of Affluence, 1951-70

The 1950s and 1960s, seen from the perspective of the present day, appear very different from one another: the former a 'stable' decade, the latter 'much more unstable' and increasingly disoriented.[1] By the early 1950s the country had recovered from the worst effects of the war and the remnants of food rationing and building controls were finally abolished in 1954. Britain experienced boom conditions arising from a seller's market both at home and abroad, but the first 'stop-go' crisis occurred in 1955-6, followed by a more serious emergency brought on by the Suez campaign. Growth resumed in the late 1950s but was subject to increasing strains associated with the 'stop-go' cycle.[2] The turning point between the 'stable' period and the 'unstable' has been variously debated, some arguing in favour of 1964 and others for 1966. As both years represent key points in the career of Harold Wilson's government — its election to power and its decision to deflate on a scale rarely before experienced in peacetime — the period 1964-6 forms a watershed in modern British history. The country was obliged to live with its consequences for many years after. It almost seemed that the Labour government was setting out to revive the austerity of the 1940s: severe financial restrictions were placed on foreign travel, purchase tax was sharply increased as were the duties on wine, spirits and tobacco. Taxes on petrol were also raised.

The British public, however, were not prepared to tolerate this kind of economic strait-jacket in peacetime; the government encountered an increasing resistance to its policies which manifested itself most alarmingly in vigorous cost-push inflation. By the early 1970s it appeared that the rate of inflation was moving out of control.

Critics of Britain's economic performance in the late 1950s and early 1960s detected a preference for 'money makers' over 'money earners.' Erratic government policy was blamed for making the country a 'speculator's paradise': 'hot money' moved in, 'brains' emigrated. The way of life of the rich and powerful was supposedly subsidised out of expense-accounts; the range of perks for management was 'constantly' extended. For everyone else there were premium bonds. Yet the better-off were apparently not satisfied: they were held to pay more tax than their equivalents in comparable countries. 'No honest man has been able to save money since the war', said Evelyn Waugh. Government policy was unable to satisfy either its supporters or its critics: there was an outcry when the Chancellor of the Exchequer raised the threshold for surtax payers from £2,000 to £4,000 in 1961 and another a year later when he introduced short-term capital gains tax.

Very little of this was reflected in the proceedings of the courts. As far as they were concerned the black economy in the 1950s and 1960s consisted of tax evasion, smuggling and pilfering with the last of far greater importance than the other two.

Theft from the employer had been a problem in British industry from the time of the First World War, if not long before. A variety of methods had been tried to suppress it. Security guards were employed (and were sometimes themselves caught stealing); the police were asked to make enquiries (they did so, arrests and prosecutions followed; pilfering continued); courts were invited to impose deterrent penalties. In 1949 a tobacco company in east London instituted a system of particularly thorough searches. Any employee caught stealing was prosecuted. Notices to this effect were put up in the factory. Old Street magistrates supported the campaign by imprisoning offenders. Yet pilfering did not cease. The editor of a local newspaper, observing these events wondered 'are we witnessing here in Stepney, a kind of parallel to the lowering of standards which went on when prohibition was enforced in the United States, another instance of a government bearing down too hard upon ordinary people concerning a normal habit. Here the trouble may well be due to the tremendous taxation on cigarettes, which has made a fairly cheap article a very expensive one ...' [3]

Within a few years the austerity of the 1940s had been succeeded by the comparative plenty of the 1950s. Shortages ceased. Wages rose in real terms. Taxation was reduced. Did any of this have an effect on pilfering? If we examine the situation at three-year intervals, beginning in 1950 and ending in 1968, we find that pilferers continued to be caught and prosecuted in considerable numbers. Birkenhead and north London still had more convictions than Walsall and Barnsley (the Brighton press no longer reported all pilfering cases). Theft from the employer was thus a feature of British industrial life whatever the general economic circumstances. If different years had been chosen, the individual totals might well have been smaller or greater but it is very unlikely that there would have been no convictions at all. It would therefore be appropriate in examining the detailed figures for these towns to speculate on the motives behind this persistent pattern of industrial behaviour.

Number of persons aged eighteen and over convicted of pilfering, 1950-68 [4]

	Barnsley	Birkenhead	N. London	Walsall
1950	4	43	98	10
1953	9	39	71	8
1956	12	46	76	7
1959	1	17	32	2
1962	2	27	65	2
1965	12	46	38	6
1968	19	15	37	12

Most of the people convicted in Barnsley were employed at only three concerns. The Co-operative Society took ten of its employees to court in 1956 and eight in 1965. The earlier group were lorry drivers and their mates and two storemen accused of stealing coal. Six people from the town were prosecuted for receiving. In 1965 eight warehouse staff were had up. One of them admitted taking goods worth £370 while two men conceded totals of £243 and £55. All eight were fined and two of them kept their jobs. They could count themselves much luckier than their predecessors in 1956.

Two of them went to jail for three months; they had stolen coal worth a few pounds.[5]

In 1968 Barnsley Canister Company and Needham Brothers between them accounted for fourteen convictions: here too the quantities of goods employees admitted stealing were sometimes considerable (including metal valued at £163 and £101). Everyone was fined.

There were thus fifty-nine convicted pilferers in Barnsley in these years. Only four were coal miners (two in 1953, one in 1965 and one in 1968). In Walsall forty-seven people were convicted but here too the names of certain firms recur: a copper works in 1953 and 1956, a glass manufacturer in 1965, a supermarket and two engineering firms in 1968. The press in both towns gave some emphasis in 1965 and 1968 to a number of large-value thefts. In Barnsley they included a night watchman who sold £200 worth of copper wire to a scrap merchant, a technical manager who disposed of £136 of platinum to a dealer in Middlesex (he paid £90 for it) and a chemical worker who arranged the sale of metal valued at several hundred pounds to a Barnsley scrapyard. In Walsall scrap metal merchants bought £240 worth of metal from a labourer for £33, and nickel turnings worth £144 from two labourers (the men admitted fourteen similar cases), while a store assistant was 'persuaded' by her boy friend to hand over stock valued at £762 and a van driver asked for sixty-eight other offences to be taken into consideration when prosecuted for stealing metal (£1,600 in all). Thefts of this size may have made other employers more alert if they read about them in the local papers. Walsall council was sufficiently alarmed to ask the town's MPs to press for a clause to be included in the West Midland parliamentary bill that would allow courts to withdraw the licences of metal dealers if they were convicted of receiving.[6] It would, however, be unsafe to generalise from these high value thefts. There were only four of them in Barnsley in 1968 and five in Walsall. In the former town fourteen thefts were of goods worth less than £16 while in the latter five people stole £10 or less, four of them goods worth under £4. Much pilfering continued to be small scale, even in cases which were taken to court.

In Birkenhead 'reported' crime in the docks decreased in

the 1950s. There were 452 offences in 1952, 370 in 1952, 345 in 1953, and only 189 in 1954. The 'preventive' watching of valuable cargoes had been re-introduced in 1952: three years later the chief constable claimed that it had 'eliminated' bulk thefts. The decline continued in the late 1950s and early 1960s, assisted by the 'mechanisation of traffic and handling equipment used on the Dock Estate'.[7] After 1964, however, 'dock crime' rose: 164 offences were reported that year, 202 in 1965 and 238 in 1966. 'Heavily dutiable goods', such as spirits and cigarettes, were particularly vulnerable.[8]

By no means all these offences were committed by dock workers. The Dock Estate was notoriously open: it had three main roads running through it from which 'access is available to almost any part of the docks'.[9] Birkenhead police reports do not provide a breakdown of the type of person prosecuted for dock thefts. From time to time they suggest that organised thieves (not dock employees) were responsible for important thefts but do not say how many were carried out by people living near the estate or who happened to be passing through. Dock labourers continued to be arrested and convicted: eighteen in 1950, eleven in 1953, twenty-six in 1956, four in 1959, twelve in 1962, twenty-two in 1965, but only two in 1968. There was no significant change in the value of individual thefts: most men took a few shillings worth of goods; at most a few pounds worth. In 1953 G. Fitzsimmons stole two tins of paint worth £2; J. Conlon two tubes of toothpaste, S. Dyer a pullover, T. Hopkins a pound of sugar. In 1956 five men were charged with stealing 300 bottles of stout: it emerged that they had drunk the lot while working on the S.S. *Grelrosa*. It was an expensive binge — the fines came to three times the cost of the bottles. In 1962 men were convicted for stealing twenty cigarettes, ten cigarettes, tubes of shaving cream, a doorbell, two tins of fish, and a bottle of whisky. Three years later men were taken through the courts and the cases duly written up in the press for stealing bottles of Horlicks, chewing gum (worth 2s), a tin of powder worth 1s, and two bottles of milk. Helping themselves to alcohol was even more expensive in 1965 than earlier: three men were fined £15 each for drinking five cans of lager. The largest value theft in 1953 was fifteen pairs of nylons worth £7 10s 0d; in 1956 it was ingots of metal worth £37. There was no significant increase in the 1960s. The biggest value theft in 1962 was carried out by a docker who put extra packages on a lorry driven by a friend. They were caught doing this with three cartons of soap worth £84 and asked for several other offences to be taken into consideration. Both were fined £100. The next largest theft was cartons of soap worth £14 and the one after that coffee and margarine worth £13. In 1965 there were two big thefts (a carton of cigarettes valued at £66 and eighty-eight bottles of whisky worth £176) but only three others worth £20 or more. Receivers continued to be conspicuous by their absence. No-one was prosecuted for receiving in relation to a dock theft in 1962, 1965 or 1968. Dockers stole for their own use, to give to friends and relatives, and perhaps also, as one man told the court, to 'hit back' at an employer.

The second largest category of workpeople arrested in Birkenhead was seamen — fifteen of them in 1953, nine in 1956, two in 1959, one in 1962 and ten in 1965. None were arrested in 1968. Few lived in the town. Several were foreigners, others were Britons whose ships had called in Birkenhead. Most stole small quantities of food or drink. A chief cook took chickens, a ship's greaser ham, an Indian seaman jars of preserves, a steward meat. Several explained that they would be staying in Birkenhead with friends and had taken the goods as a contribution to their board.[10] The remaining pilferers arrested numbered between eleven and seventeen in every year except 1956 when there were only four. Many of these seventy-one people worked for a small number of employers: Norman Foods (seven), the National Coal Board (nine lorry drivers), Cammell Laird's (ten), Threlfall's brewery (four), British Road Services and British Railways (five). Nineteen of them were lorry or van drivers. Very few took more than a few pounds' worth of goods and only three more than £20 worth. The first of these three was a labourer at Alison's, the ship repairer's. He sold £327 worth of brass fittings to a metal dealer who paid him £10. This man had a record for theft and receiving and was the only person convicted of receiving pilfered goods in 1956.

The others were two eighteen-year-old labourers at Cammell's who sold metal worth £138 to a metal dealer. He reported them to the police saying they gave him a different name every time they came to him with metal.[11]

Even in north London it is hard to detect evidence of an organised black economy in the 1950s and not very much easier for the 1960s. There were seven thefts of goods worth more than £30 in 1950, four in 1953, eleven in 1956 and only two in 1959. Those concerned included two young men who stole shoes (£160 worth) and 'carried on a business with the proceeds'; a warehouseman who overloaded a lorry with Truman's beers which the driver sold to a pub manager — the police arrived in time to catch the manager paying the driver £4 for a consignment worth £9;[12] a lorry driver who sold £200 worth of furniture (including five tables and twenty-eight bureaus) to a tradesman — the police spotted the property in his shop. The price they agreed was £100 but the driver complained that he was still owed £18.[13]

Very few people were convicted of receiving: three in 1953, seven in 1956, four in 1959 while even fewer were tradesmen (a café proprietor in 1953, a radio dealer and a scrap metal merchant in 1956, two public house licensees in 1959). Seventeen people had been selling the goods they pilfered but not many were as organised about it as Maurice Lazarus, an electrician at Whitbread's. He took stolen electrical goods to Club Row and laid them out for sale on the pavement. There was 'a considerable quantity', enough to attract the interest of the police.[14]

About a quarter of the pilferers in each of these years stole cloth or clothing, but cigarettes were now taken less frequently. Magistrates believed this was because of improved security and tougher sentencing but equally important may have been the increasingly generous allowance of 'free' cigarettes that employers included in workers' pay.

Lorry drivers were arrested more often: they accounted for two pilferers in every five convicted in 1959 compared to one in five in 1953. In Birkenhead one driver was arrested in 1953, two in 1956 and five in 1959. A London magistrate decided, on the basis of figures like these, that drivers were 'subject to the most appalling temptations if they were ready to make money on the side'.[15] The 1950s, of course, saw a substantial increase in the amount of road traffic and the quantity of goods carried by lorry. In 1953 the railways accounted for 54 per cent of the volume of freight and road for 46 per cent.[16] Nine years later rail took only 32 per cent, the rest went by road. Road transport firms had also been tightening up their security.

Systematic pilfering was hardly of greater significance in the 1960s than it had been in the previous decade. In 1962 a storekeeper and a tyre fitter sold 280 stolen tyres, making £550 between them. Their employers discovered what was happening from invoices. Both men were jailed. In the same year a storeman sold £1,200 of cloth in a series of deals to a man describing himself as 'a director'; they were also jailed. So were two drivers and a warehouseman who sold £350 worth of confectionery to a grocer. In 1965 a checker at Hanson Haulage was questioned by a security officer about a jacket he was wearing. He admitted he had stolen it from the firm. Questioned further he admitted that he 'picked out' goods (mainly cloth) and gave them to two of the company's drivers. They sold them to a driver with another firm: nearly £400 of goods had gone.[17] In 1968 a driver for the publisher's, Hamlyn's, sold £800 worth of books to another van driver. His home was searched and the police found forty-four pairs of trousers, 164 packets of razor blades, and 1,700 contraceptives. They said they had difficulty finding out where all this property came from: a thirty-six-year-old man would presumably not have been so eccentric as to buy it for his own use. Cases like these headed press reports about court proceedings but they were no more typical of north London pilfering in the 1960s than similar cases had been of previous decades. Only five people were convicted of receiving pilfered goods in 1962 (all of them tradesmen), three in 1965 (two were grocers) and three in 1968 (all were workfellows of the pilferers). One pilferer in ten sold goods in 1965 and one in five in 1962 and 1968. Many more stole goods of small value.[18]

The great majority lost their jobs and few employers spoke up for them in court. Nine out of ten lost their jobs in 1953 and 1956 while in 1959 only one man was kept on. Among the minority was a motor driver who stole £6 worth of quilts. His employer told the magistrate 'whether you fine him – if he cannot pay I will pay for him – or whether you put him in prison, and I hope you won't . . . when he comes out I will take him back'. He even offered to pay the fine which the magistrate imposed, but that was not allowed.[19] Another employer the same year wanted to drop a charge against two workpeople who had stolen shirts. The magistrate refused his permission for that but he put one man on probation and conditionally discharged the other. Three years later the employer of a lorry driver appearing in court for the sixth time on a pilfering charge 'spoke very highly of him' and offered him his job back.[20] In 1962 the magistrate in a case in which three young men were charged with stealing £25 worth of wood listened as their employer told them they would keep their jobs. He fined them £50 each adding that he 'did not understand why a firm . . . should want to take back employees who had stolen from them'.[21] There may of course have been more to the relationships that lay behind these comments than courts could ever know about. In Birkenhead every pilferer prosecuted between 1953 and 1968 lost his job.

Between 1953 and 1968 there was a tendency for a greater proportion of arrests for pilfering to take place at work.

Number of arrests in north London

	at work	elsewhere
1953	7	15
1956	12	19
1959	7	9
1962	7	9
1965	10	5
1968	9	2

In 1953 all the people caught at work were railway or tobacco workers while in 1956 six of the twelve were arrested in December when some firms made special checks to prevent people stealing for Christmas presents. In 1962 five other arrests were made as a result of 'information' reaching the police. In 1965 there were two such and in 1968 six. Police rarely revealed much about their sources on these occasions. These numbers are too small to allow very much to be made of them but it is interesting to note that the same tendency emerged in the provincial towns. No pilferer in Walsall or Barnsley was arrested away from work in 1962, 1965 or 1968. This change may reflect the rise in the number of people travelling to and from work by motor transport which was much more difficult to stop and search than when people went to work on foot. Arrests in the 1960s were thus in a much higher proportion of cases than previously the result of an initiative by an employer. This had of course been the position in Birkenhead throughout.

During the 1950s and 1960s sentencing practice diverged between north London and the provincial towns. In Birkenhead two offenders in five had been jailed in 1950. In 1953 no-one was jailed while in 1956 only four people were.[22] No-one was jailed in 1959 while the two who were in 1962 were both security men.[23] No pilferer was imprisoned in 1965 but in 1968 two eighteen-year-olds who had stolen and sold metal from Cammell Laird's were sent to a detention centre for three months. (Both security men caught pilfering were fined. One, who had a previous conviction for stealing, stole seven packets of chewing gum worth 7d; the other one stole dog food worth £72.)

In Walsall three of the eight pilferers convicted in 1953 were jailed but they were not followed by anyone else in later years. In Barnsley a man with a record of six offences was jailed for a year in 1953 and three more were imprisoned in 1956. Thereafter no-one went inside.

In north London two pilferers in five were jailed in 1950, one in three in 1953, one in six in 1956 and 1959. In 1962 the proportion was one in three and in 1965 two in five. The contrast between the provincial towns and north London was becoming very marked and may be illustrated by some examples. In Walsall in 1962 a man who stole a water heater was fined £15; a labourer who sold £240 worth of metal to a scrapdealer (the man paid him £33) was fined £40 — the labourer also kept his job. In Barnsley a bricklayer took window and door frames and put them into a pair of semi-detached bungalows he was building. The court fined him

£25; nor did his employer give him the sack. A night watch-man who sold £200 worth of copper wire was fined £40. And so on. In north London in these years magistrates jailed for three months a labourer who took 234 cigarettes, a driver who stole a carton of handbags and a labourer who took metal worth £7 10s 0d. A young woman who stole cosmetics which did not amount in value to so much as £5 went inside for one month, and a warehouseman who stole £47 worth of alcohol was jailed for six months. In 1962 a number of pil-ferers were remanded in custody for reports. A labourer who had stolen ninety glasses worth £3 15s 0d was remanded in custody for four weeks and then conditionally discharged;[24] an employee at Hackney Hospital who had taken pork chops worth 10s 0d was remanded in custody for two days before also being conditionally discharged.[25] Two young men who stole a few pounds worth of goods were remanded in custody for a fortnight. It would seem that the traditional court system continued to be poorly suited to dealing with economic offences. The independence of the bench and the failure of magistrates to find out what was happening elsewhere meant that marked contrasts in sentencing emerged. The never-ending procession of pilferers through the courts showed that they had failed to suppress it. Remarks pilferers made suggest that many of them persisted in regarding theft from the employer as in effect 'a perk': it only became 'a crime' if the goods were sold. The approach of employers to the problem was not consistent, some prosecuted offenders, others did not, still others made a separate decision for each pilferer. Of three people caught on the same occasion, one might be prosecuted and keep his job, another be taken to court and also lose his job while the third might get off with a warning. This was bound to add to the sense of ambiguity about the precise legal status of theft from the employer. If magistrates wanted to remove it, it was essential that they sentence consistently. Tribunals, following clear lines of policy, might have been able to do so, but magistrates con-tinued to have wide powers of discretion. Hence in the 1960s Barnsley and Walsall benches were reluctant to jail offenders while the bench in north London imprisoned them relatively often. But even there variations occurred between courts and magistrates. In 1953 one magistrate at Old Street court, H.F.R. Sturge, jailed eight out of seventeen offenders who appeared before him whereas another, Leslie Marks, jailed four out of thirteen.[26] In 1962 and 1965 N.M. McElligott at Old Street jailed ten pilferers out of twenty-three while Frank Milton at North London jailed two out of ten.[26] Faced with a 29-year-old man who had stolen and sold a carton of jars of onions and who had five previous convictions Milton fined him and the receiver, a grocer, £20 each. McElligott, meanwhile, sentenced a twenty-two-year-old labourer, who had stolen 234 cigarettes, to three months. In 1965 he sentenced a coalman, who had sold coke to a public house, to twelve months; and a fifty-three-year-old cleaner who had taken £10 worth of goods to six months. One month later a BRS driver charged with selling an overload (a parcel) to a greengrocer appeared before Milton. He fined him £25.[27] And so on. It may be objected that magistrates were swayed by the specific circumstances of each case — the appearance and demeanour of the prisoner, the fluency of the defending counsel if there was one, the comments made by the employer or his representative — in arriving at such different sentences. But the danger is that the law itself may be brought into disrepute if some people are jailed and others not for very similar offences. There is evidence to suggest that workmates of pilferers paid close attention to what happened to them. In Birkenhead docks when a labourer was arrested for theft his workmates took a collection to pay the fine.[28] People taken to court were often able to refer to the judgment in previous cases involving workfellows. During both world wars pilferers had been jailed more frequently than black marketeers. In peacetime, too, courts tended to take a more lenient view when employers broke the law than when employees did. For instance, in October 1953, United Dairies was prosecuted for 'distributing' a milk bottle that was not in a 'thorough state of cleanliness'. A customer had complained about the dirty milk bottle left at her house and inquiries revealed that United Dairies had four previous convictions for this offence at North London court alone. The magistrate, Frank Powell, none the less fined the company £2: 'considering the millions of bottles they filled it was a very good record.'[29]

One month later a bakehouse and flour store were prosecuted by Hackney council. Food was prepared for human consumption on premises which inspectors found to be 'indescribably filthy'. Troughs in the bakehouse were 'infested' with weevils, cockroaches and moths; the condition of the walls was 'very, very bad indeed'. The owners had been given several previous verbal and written warnings, but six weeks after the last of these the inspectors decided that court action must be taken. Having heard the evidence the magistrate Seymour Collins said: 'I don't want to do anything likely to put a one-man businessman out of business . . . I think they should be encouraged rather than that we should have to buy bread from multiple stores or multiple bakeries. . . . It may be that you make better bread but it must be clean.' He fined the owner of the establishment £9.[30] That very same week he remanded an eighteen-year-old youth in custody for seven days for a medical report because he had stolen a piece of cloth worth £4.[31]

It may be objected that offences against the health laws and theft from the employer should not be compared but a worker reading the *Hackney Gazette* may not have noticed such subtleties. To him it may well have seemed that there was one law 'for the bosses' and another for everyone else.

By 1968 parliament itself had intervened to restrict the jailing of workpeople who had stolen from their employers. Not all magistrates were entirely happy with the change. When a security officer at Lesney's with a 'good' character appeared before McElligott and was charged with stealing £7 worth of toys, the magistrate imposed a twelve-month prison sentence, suspended for three years, and a £200 fine. Even so he complained that parliament gave him no alternative. 'His view was that the security officer ought to go to prison forthwith.'[32] Yet the problem of contrasts in sentencing remained. On the same day that he heard the case against the security man at Lesney's, McElligott had to decide in a case against two workmen at Stanton's Pure Products. They had stolen a stove which made toffee apples and used it to 'set up in business themselves'. Their employer discovered what was happening when toffee apples not made by Stanton's were found to be wrapped in their paper. One of the

men had seven previous convictions yet McElligott fined him
£50. He conditionally discharged the other.[33] Depending
which magistrate heard the case the theft of a few pounds
worth of goods could be punished by a fine of £5 or £50.
A jail sentence of six months suspended for three years was
imposed by McElligott on a canteen worker who stole bacon
worth 2s 6d, yet two men both with records were fined £40
each for stealing a hair drier valued at £57 which they tried
to sell. The magistrate in this case, Graham-Hall, did not
impose suspended sentences.

Motives for pilfering seem to have been almost as various
as the goods that were taken. The idea that the goods they
had made were in some part the property of those who made
them was expressed from time to time. It is clear that many
pilferers did not know what to do with pilfered property
once they got it out of the factory. 'I don't know what makes
me do it', said a porteress at Boots in Barnsley. 'I did not
really need any of the articles.' An electrician who had taken
electrical equipment worth £14 said he stole for 'no special
purpose. I was just collecting it.' Considerable quantities of
property were found when police visited pilferers' homes:
they had made no attempt to sell it. One man had £95 worth
of Christmas crackers, another £31 worth of carbon paper,
another nearly a hundred mirrors, yet another £875 worth
of kitchen equipment. The firm this man worked for had
recently been taken over and had stopped paying a bonus
of £60 a year: he said he had 'a grudge' against them as a
result. A grievance against the employer was mentioned
often: a Barnsley warehouseman took £319 worth of property to 'spite' his 'boss'.[34] Others were going to be made
redundant, still others complained that the pay was too
low. Magistrates sometimes heard them sympathetically.[35]
Still others saw that pilfering was going on generally and
joined in. One man parcelled up £350 worth of wireless valves
and posted them to himself. All the property was found at
his home. A director of the firm 'had a great personal regard
for him. He was the last man he would have suspected.'
The man explained that the company was 'so badly organised
. . . that thieving went on openly. He turned his back on
temptation for a long time, but after he had been there a year

. . . he said to himself "What's good for the other employees is good for me." '[36] 'I saw others taking them,' said a Christmas stocking filler, 'so I took some myself.' Still others claimed that pressure was brought to bear on employees who did not steal. If you did not join in you were 'out'.

As we have seen a minority of pilferers took goods to sell them and a few organised what they were doing with considerable skill, but most took for their own use or to give away. A laundry worker stole towels and linen because she 'had just started a new home and had to start from scratch. I did not consider it was stealing.'[37] Others gave goods to friends: £54 worth of wool, eighteen harmonicas, bicycle chains, wood, shoes, chocolates — and were presumably eventually given something in return. As Madeleine Kerr noted of the people she studied in Ship Street, Liverpool: 'On the whole there is a lot of "obliging". Our Bert has a job where he has access to some commodity someone wants. It's a waste to buy it in the shops where it is so expensive. He takes a small quantity and gives it. He in turn will then be obliged with something he wants. . . . In neither of these instances is money used, and there is no consciousness of law-breaking.'[38]

At the same time very few people charged with theft from the employer contested the charges against them. Before the Second World War it was most unusual for a defendant to plead not guilty. In north London one did so in 1932, two in 1934 and none at all in 1937. Most, of course, were caught 'bang to rights' (that is, with the stolen goods on their person); occasionally someone would insist that they had been 'planted' by an 'enemy'. In 1941 six people pleaded not guilty and three did so in 1944. In Birkenhead the proportion was slightly higher: one in ten in 1941 and one in eight in 1944. Nor did the position change much in the 1950s and 1960s: one north London defendant pleaded not guilty in 1953 but none at all did so in the other years, while in Birkenhead there was one in 1953, one in 1962 and three in 1965. It is surprising that after more than fifty years of rapid social change and supposedly increasing self-confidence on the part of the working class, so few should have fought the case against them. The overwhelming majority were not legally represented in court.

Pilfering remained throughout an offence carried out mainly by males, despite the large entry of women into the labour market after the end of the Second World War. In Birkenhead this is not surprising given the predominance of dock workers among pilferers. No woman was convicted in 1917 and only two in 1919 (both laundry workers). Two were convicted in 1962 (petrol pump attendants who put petrol into their own cars), three in 1965 (shop assistants), but none in 1968. In north London, an area with traditionally high recruitment into the clothing industry, the proportion of convicted pilferers who were females in 1968 (8 per cent) was lower than it had been in 1917 (26 per cent). Six women were convicted in 1953 (out of seventy-one), six in 1956 (out of seventy-six) and three in 1959 (out of thirty-two). The position did not change in the following decade. Five women were convicted in 1962, five in 1965 and three in 1968.

The remaining groups of people involved in the black economy who fell foul of the authorities were tax evaders and smugglers. In these towns both groups represented a small and diminishing band. If we examine the position between 1953 and 1968 at three-year intervals we find that only six people were prosecuted for tax evasion. Five were purchase-tax offenders and the sixth a Walsall bookmaker who had evaded paying betting tax. He was fined £240 in 1968 for failing to disclose that he had a number of credit customers.[39]

The purchase-tax offenders were small businessmen in north London: two tailors, a jeweller, a printer, and a leather goods manufacturer. The amount of tax evaded was tiny: business difficulties the usual explanation. Only one of them was fined over £250. These people were in a slightly bigger way of business than the tradesmen who still occasionally were taken to court for failing to buy health and insurance stamps for their employees. But both groups could hardly be further removed from the tax avoiders who were to cause the tax authorities such concern in the early 1970s. Fines imposed barely covered the costs of prosecution.

Very few smugglers were prosecuted in these years. In Birkenhead nineteen people were convicted, fifteen of them seamen. Three were British, the rest mainly Europeans. They were caught with small quantities of cigarettes, watches, alcohol or nylons, usually discovered when customs officers searched the ship on which they worked. No evidence was produced in court to suggest that they were assisting anyone else, though several said they had intended to sell the goods once they got them ashore. Fines were imposed in all cases, the highest £150.

Only four people were prosecuted for dealing in smuggled goods. A Birkenhead market stall-holder was fined £40 for selling US nylons he had bought from a cook on the S.S. *Franconia* in 1953.[40] Three years later a labourer bought watches from a seaman and sold them to a shopkeeper. Fourteen watches were mentioned in the charges and the two men were fined £25 each.[41] In 1965 the room of a Greek Cypriot was searched and 5,000 cigarettes and a box containing thirteen bottles of brandy were found. He said he had exchanged them for cloth with the crew of a Greek ship. He was fined £100.[42] Police reports for Birkenhead mention only one serious instance of smuggling for the period between 1945 and 1966.[43] This occurred in 1963 when six Burmese seamen were arrested on board ship with 13 lbs of Indian hemp which was said to be worth £12,000 on the drug market.

In north London, too, cigarettes, watches and nylons were the goods smuggled most often though the quantities were larger than in Birkenhead. In 1953 customs officers visited a thirty-one-year-old company director at his place of work and found two bags with Italian diplomatic seals. They contained 2,100 Swiss watches. The company director was said by police to be a receiver of smuggled goods on 'an international scale': an Italian courier brought watches from Paris on behalf of 'a gang' in the French capital.[44] In 1956 a father and son were arrested in Stamford Hill in possession of £35,000 worth of watches; in 1959 the son was caught again, this time with £20,000 worth. In that year a Hungarian refugee was found to have nearly 6,000 watches, brought to him by an Air France mechanic. All these men were jailed for terms up to eighteen months.[45] Six other were prosecuted for smuggling smaller quantities of goods (cigars or watches). Most described themselves as watch-repairers or jewellers, though one was a dressmaker and one a leather goods manufacturer. All but three were foreigners, several were stateless persons or refugees. They were too few in number and the goods they smuggled too small in quantity to constitute a significant black economy.

7

The Modern Black Economy

This study of the black economy has shown that as far as the towns surveyed here were concerned it was usually small-scale: very few cases were of more than local significance. A 'market' was not created in any product and the authorities never lost control of the situation. In case after case in which prosecutors spoke of the seriousness of what had happened and judges and magistrates commented accordingly, the evidence shows that the goods or sums of money involved were invariably trivial — 166 head of cattle, overcharges amounting to several hundred pounds, 500 smuggled watches, pilfered foodstuffs 'which might well have stocked a small shop', tax evaded totalling £1,500. In the few instances which developed beyond this — share-pushing in the 1930s, the black market in petrol in the 1940s — determined action by the authorities defeated the threat.

During the First World War the government responded slowly to a growing economic crisis and during 1916 and 1917 the black market emerged. During 1918 the government acted with determination, brought the domestic economy under control and the black market with it. The most serious difficulty lay in securing a consistent response in the courts. Variations occurred in sentencing from one area to another. Different categories of offence tended to be punished differently: businessmen's crimes by fines, workmen's crimes by jail. This would have been an appropriate moment to consider whether economic offences should be sent to a new form of court, perhaps a tribunal, which would have been able to make the use of the knowledge of experts. But the possibility was not considered, then or later. The traditional system of justice continued to function and black marketeers, tax evaders and pilferers were prosecuted in the same courts as burglars and housebreakers, sexual offenders, and those charged with crimes of violence.

The black market did not cease with the end of the war. Controls were still needed. The law was broken often and offenders continued to be taken to court in large numbers. But the black market had little effect on patterns of organised theft and pilfering and never achieved the dimensions reached by contemporary continental black markets. With the onset of depression, prices and ·wages fell, demand slackened and the black market faded.

The prolonged depression of the inter-war period produced different forms of black economic activity. Long-firm frauds took advantage of the poor business climate to obtain and sell illicitly goods secured on credit; small businessmen and retailers sought to evade health and insurance tax in order, they claimed, to keep their firms solvent; share-pushers siphoned off large sums of capital into bogus get-rich-quick schemes. Yet the sums of money raised from tax evasion were derisory; the long-firm cases I have been able to trace rarely involved large sums of money (only one received goods worth more than £4,000); share-pushers were the subject of a government enquiry. The authorities may have been slow to respond to the challenge but once they did so they were effective.

In the Second World War controls were introduced ahead of the anticipated eruption of the black market and were enforced with determination throughout. Organised theft expanded above the low pre-war levels but most thefts from the employer continued to be carried out for personal use, not to supply the black economy. Tax evasion almost ceased to be matter for the courts and allegations that it was growing did not find corroboration there.

Black marketeering did not end with the war any more than it had in 1918. Indeed manifestations of serious black market activity rose to their highest levels in 1947 and 1948 but in only one product, petrol, did 'a market' show signs of emerging. The authorities reacted strongly and a government spokesman felt able to claim that the black market in petrol had been defeated. But the experience was disturbing, showing what might happen if public patience with rationing and shortages became utterly exhausted. There was a danger that organised criminals might move into the gap. The late 1940s was the most favourable moment in modern British history for this to happen — akin to the American experience of prohibition. However, Britain's criminals did not possess the powers of organisation, identity of interest, or violent ruthlessness of the American Mafia. Even if they had it seems highly improbable that public opinion would have let them get away with it. The period of danger passed when the country's economic equilibrium was restored and austerity brought to an end. By 1951 the worst shortages had ceased and the government was able to start 'a bonfire of controls'.

Thereafter the main forms of black economic activity were pilfering, smuggling and tax evasion. The authorities concentrated most of their energy on the former. It is likely that this reflects the comparative significance of the first two — smuggling was a fringe activity in the 1950s and 1960s — but tax evasion was frequently said to be widespread. As we have seen, such claims found little reflection in the courts. It may be that here, as in share-pushing in the 1930s, a long period passed before the authorities were alerted to the full seriousness of what was going on. The resulting uproar, accompanied by somewhat frenzied attempts to find answers, occurred during the 1970s.

Although this study has not found evidence of a substantial black economy it has shown that in these towns the relevant laws were broken often and many small-scale transactions took place. Indeed considerable energy and ingenuity were devoted to the black economy. Disproportionate risks were taken to obtain almost trivial benefits. Shopkeepers chanced arrest, conviction and the likelihood of bad publicity for a few pounds' worth of overcharges, pilferers risked jail to obtain a few shillings' worth of goods. The disparity between the likely advantage and the danger is so great that it seems probable that many black economy transactions did not have only an economic motive. They also fended off boredom ('fiddling at work gives the job an interest', said Alfie in the film of that name), and scored points against employers, the taxman, and business partners.

Many pilferers saw pilfering as a working man's perk, the equivalent of the company car and the expense account lunch. Perhaps companies did so too. J. P. Martin, in his study of Reading, found that three-quarters of forty-nine larger firms in the town and an 'even higher' proportion of forty-eight smaller ones provided circumstances in which they agreed it would be 'quite easy' or 'very easy' for workers to steal from the firm.[1] So if the employer decided suddenly to crack down, a strong reaction could follow. In 1946, seventeen hundred men employed at Bishopsgate goods depôt went on strike when two of them were charged with stealing tomatoes. They complained that the company could have used 'disciplinary action' instead of 'dragging the men's names through the courts'.[2] Twenty-seven years later 200 men at BL's Longbridge plant walked out. They said they were being 'harassed' by visits from West Midland police looking for stolen car components.[3]

J. P. Martin questioned whether *not* calling in the police in cases of pilfering was in the public interest. Many employers combined a policy of prosecuting pilferers with continuing to employ them. Nearly one-third of the men in the larger firms in his sample who were prosecuted in fact kept their jobs. But when employers used their discretion in such cases they were in effect taking the law into their own hands. The victim of the crime was making himself counsel, judge and jury in his own cause.[4]

The black economy thus raises questions about social justice. Throughout our period the authorities have been more consistent in trying to suppress the working-class crime of pilfering than they have the white-collar crime of tax evasion. In both world wars, jail sentences had been imposed far more freely on working-class offenders than on businessmen and shopkeepers who broke the law. The 1970s would see whether this bias continued to prevail, as tax evasion became the aspect of the black economy most in the public eye.

Between 1964 and 1970 the Labour government had been faced with a fundamental dilemma: what was to be the relationship between its social policy and the level of taxation? Could advances in the first be reconciled with stability in the second or would a choice have to be made? In fact the government's mishandling of the economy was so serious that it suffered the worst of all possible worlds. Social policy was compromised while taxation rose. The government failed to work out the implications of imposing higher taxes, especially on the rich, and did not strengthen the supervisory machinery to defeat evasion. The Inland Revenue had to devote all its resources to catching up on the backlog of work caused by previous budget changes. The danger was that more revenue would be lost by the growth in evasion than the government stood to gain by its tax increases.

Even before Harold Wilson came to power tax levels were felt by many to be too high. Under the previous Labour government in 1951 the top rate of tax had been 91½ per cent and anyone earning £15,000 or over paid 19s 6d in the pound on his top slice of earnings. While the Conservatives were in office (1951 to 1964) the standard rate of tax had been reduced from 9s 6d in the pound to 7s 9d, and the top rate to 88¾ per cent. After 1964 taxes returned to higher levels: standard income tax to 8s 3d and the top tax rate to 91¼ per cent. Indirect taxes were also drastically increased, especially in the post-devaluation budgets of April and November 1968. The impact of these changes on the Inland Revenue was that 'the chance of getting a reply from the revenue within a reasonable period is remote, that a high proportion of assessments are incorrect, that large numbers of people are entitled to repayments they do not receive, that the policing of returns is elementary and that there can be no reliable estimate of the potential taxpayers who neither make, nor are called upon to make, disclosure of their income.'[5]

During the late 1960s the rate of inflation showed a worrying tendency to rise at an accelerating rate. The cause was controversial but the results seemed clear. From 1968 to 1970 retail prices rose by an average of 5.9 per cent a year whilst the rise between 1970 and 1973 was 8.6 per cent a year.[6] Data assembled by the Treasury suggested that there was a 'a correlation' between inflation and taxation. A comparative study of the OECD countries showed that 'inflation has often been most rampant since 1964 where tax increases had been sharpest'. Britain and Sweden headed the list. In 1970, it was suggested, the tax burden in Great Britain was heavier than it had been even in 1946.[7]

Growing numbers of people were looking for ways to avoid paying tax. Many workers in the service sector sought employment in the evenings and at weekends for which they would be paid in cash. When Sir Lawrence Airey, chairman of the board of Inland Revenue, admitted that he paid his window cleaner in cash at least one newspaper photographer tried to get a picture of him. My landlady, when I first moved to London, insisted that the rent be paid in cash, not by cheque. Twenty tenants lived in that house and she owned another two in Chelsea. During the 1960s and 1970s such transactions became more numerous yet they are difficult to trace and it is impossible to say how much tax was lost. One clue lay in the tendency of large bank notes to slip out of the formal economy. The Bank of England had difficulty in withdrawing old large denomination notes from circulation and regained less than half. *The Economist* (22 September 1979) suggested that such notes never passed through a bank or any other financial institution.

The expense of prosecution did not make it worthwhile financially to take many of these people to court. This was not so with tax evasion by the rich yet, almost incredibly, the first group to receive sustained attention from the tax authorities was not the wealthy, but workmen – the 'lump' in the building industry, so-called because casual labourers had traditionally been paid a lump sum for their work. It was widely felt that pay policies were encouraging workers to join the lump in order to avoid the impact of pay ceilings, and men 'on the lump' by 1973 accounted for over 25 per cent of the workforce on building sites and included skilled men like bricklayers and plasterers. The practice was spreading to other industries, especially among electricians, carpenters and haulage drivers (it was discovered that drivers of heavy vehicles had become 'unaccountably' scarce). The number of self-employed temporary typists was also increasing fast. Whereas the median rate for secretaries was £1,500 at this time, salaries of £3,500 were required to attract newcomers.

The lump was opposed by 'the big battalions' on both sides of the industry: the trades union and the larger building companies. They argued that the lump recruited only skilled workers and did not provide any training for novices; it created local labour monopolies on building sites because lump labour worked as a gang rather than as individuals and was therefore able to bid up the general level of wages on the site; and, finally, no-one assumed responsibility for such matters as safety and insurance. The resistance came from lump labour itself and from the smaller house builders, many of whom were former 'lump' men. They preferred to employ lump labour because it kept their responsibility for the workforce to a minimum and encouraged fast work as all pay was by the piece. The result was that at a time when pay policy restricted pay increases to an average of 8 per cent, the earnings of building workers rose by 50 per cent.

Anthony Barber's first budget had introduced a new rule that men on the lump must produce a tax exemption certificate before they were paid. If they did not do this the building firm was obliged to deduct 30 per cent from their pay and send it directly to the Inland Revenue. This was thought to be 'penal treatment' as the employee lost his personal allowances. To any student of the black market in the 1940s, however, the next stage was predictable: the growth of a minor industry which set out to forge these certificates. Two years later it was clear that something had gone wrong and the authorities were obliged to introduce a certificate that was harder to forge and more difficult to obtain (an astonishing 400,000 of them had been granted). They also moved to close another loophole in the law whereby the lump labourer had avoided having to produce the exemption certificate by registering himself as a limited company. As this cost only about £100, numerous building workers — and others — had taken advantage of it. It was decided that there would be no exemption in future for limited companies.

The new certificate was a more formidable document than its predecessor. If a sub-contractor wanted to be paid gross he had to obtain a form 714 which showed that he had paid his full entitlement of tax for the previous three years. Form 714 was a plastic card complete with a photograph which was thought to be impossible to forge. If he was unable to produce this form he was paid net of basic tax. The fear of losing '714' status apparently kept certificated sub-contractors in line while deductions at source for uncertificated ones boosted tax recovery. The Construction Industry Manpower Board estimated that the size of the lump had declined 'significantly' between 1974 and 1977, though there had also been a recession in the building industry during that period.[8]

The Inland Revenue also launched investigations into companies which had broken the tax laws. J. Murphy, a north London subsidiary of the London and Northern Group, was successfully prosecuted and fined £675,000, while three top-level executives were jailed for three years. An inquiry into the William Press group, however, ran into greater difficulties, as will be seen.

The Heath government struggled throughout its period of office to reduce the rate of inflation, mainly by means of wage and price policies, but with no long-term success: the rate was 9.2 per cent in 1972-3, but 16 per cent in 1973-4.[9] The oil crisis at the end of 1973 and the confrontation with the miners that winter destroyed the government and Labour returned to power in early 1974. Inflation during that and the following year rose to 24.1 per cent, and by 1975 retail prices were 175 per cent higher than they had been in 1963. High-level incomes were said to be particularly hard hit. It was estimated in 1974 that if a person earning £10,000 a year wanted to maintain his or her living standards over the next four years he would have to boost his earnings to £40,000 a year by 1978, assuming that inflation continued at the 1974 level. This was clearly impossible. *The Economist* summed up the way many people were thinking at this time: 'The only practical way [a middle-class man] can really defend himself and his family is to become independent and get a till to live out of. This means becoming self-employed . . . If he manages it, he will be able to claim as tax deductable at least a part of those middle-class costs which otherwise must be paid out of net taxed income. If he can get control of his cash receipts he will, within limits, be able to help himself — as he (and everyone else) knows perfectly well that many more shopkeepers do.' Or, alternatively, 'there's always a tax haven in the Channel Islands.'[10]

The new Labour government did not propose to bring any relief to the better-off: quite the reverse. It was committed to introducing a wealth tax and a capital transfer tax. The latter was intended to stop a loophole in estate duty — a tax that was 'notoriously' easy to avoid — by making lifetime gifts subject to tax at the same rate as at death. Critics suggested that this would prevent people making substantial gifts during their lifetime and would hit small businesses and farms especially hard. The government offered a concession, proposing to reduce the tax liability on transfers of wealth made more than three years before death, but its critics were still not satisfied, while the proposed wealth tax raised a storm of protest.

Fears were expressed, especially in the Inland Revenue, that both taxes and the measures taken to enforce them (a strengthened inspectorate with greater powers) would provoke a middle-class 'backlash'. There was a growing tendency on the part of the government in the mid 1970s to employ extra bureaucrats to police the varying forms of tax evasion: it was also proposed to introduce a 700-strong body of inspectors to investigate the lump.[11] Some people questioned whether such measures, which recalled the wartime inspectorates of the Board of Trade and the Ministry of Food, could be justified in peacetime, even for so serious a problem as tax evasion.

Meanwhile, manifestations of a 'middle-class backlash' were detected. In 1974 the National Association of Ratepayers' Action Groups had been formed and claimed a paper total of thirteen million members. In the following year GB 75 was established, joining the Middle Class Association (later renamed the Voice of the Independent Centre) and Unison (founded by General Sir Walter Walker and renamed Civil Assistance in 1974). They proclaimed that their purpose was to defend the interests of a threatened middle class. Much brouhaha followed and some saw in them a dangerous paramilitary threat. There was particular suspicion of the '100 per cent anti-Communist propaganda' of their leading spokesmen.

Troops were available, some believed, in security firms. The total manpower of the private security industry amounted to 100,000 in 1977, a force of about the same size as the police. The 'private armies' of the security firms could become 'the private armies of the Right'.[12] However, the middle-class pressure groups did not manage a sustained existence. GB 75 collapsed before 1975 was over, while the Voice of the Independent Centre became the victim of disputes among its leaders. They were a manifestation of the loss of confidence in the Conservative Party, the traditional vehicle for middle-class protest. When Mrs Thatcher succeeded Edward Heath as leader and the party moved significantly to the right, many people who had been attracted to one of the new organisations returned to their old allegiance.

The government's proposed wealth tax had eventually to be abandoned when the Labour Party lost its majority in the House of Commons; it was pointed out that even so, the Chancellor of the Exchequer, Denis Healey, had raised taxation by £1¼ billion in his budget of 1975. Of greater and more lasting importance were two other connected developments which came into their own in the 1970s: the tax avoidance industry and off-shore tax havens such as the Channel Islands and the Isle of Man.

As taxes rose and with them both avoidance and the 'policing' of avoidance, increasing numbers of business and financial concerns and wealthy individuals sought to protect their investments by transferring them to a tax haven.

The economy of the Channel Islands had traditionally relied on agriculture, horticulture and tourism: by the late 1970s finance had joined them. In 1980 tourism contributed 38 per cent and finance 25 per cent of Jersey's tax revenue; one year later the proportions were 35 per cent each.[13] Until about 1960 the main Manx industries had been farming, fishing and tourism, all in decline. During the 1960s the island's government became increasingly aware of the skilful way the Channel Islands had made use of their status as crown dependencies (semi-independent English-speaking states) to attract investments from all over the world. Undoubtedly the Channel Islands were assisted by their favourable geographical situation: although the Manxmen could not compete with that they could offer equal tax advantages. In the early 1960s the level of income tax was reduced and incentives for financiers and investors were provided. Advertisements in the British and international press pointed out that there was no wealth or surtax, no exchange controls, no corporation or capital gains tax. A 'priceless asset', was 'over 1,000 years of political stability'. Panama, Monaco and Liechtenstein could hardly compete with that while even the Channel Islands had been invaded during the Second World War. In 1969-70 finance accounted for 12.4 per cent of Manx income; in 1977-78 it provided 29 per cent and had become the island's most important single activity.[14] The island's future as a tax haven was secured when the House of Lords ruled in March 1981 that the British Inland Revenue had no power to investigate Manx bank records, even when the banks were primarily British ones. Confidentiality is a prime factor in successful tax havens and this was now assured. Documents deposited within the island's jurisdiction were safe from prying British eyes.[15]

The result is that two British economies now exist, one on the mainland, the other on the islands. The growing prosperity of the latter is based on their ability to protect investments and deposits from the former: they are in effect parasitic on the mainland economy.[16] Ease of transit, the absence of language barriers and a 'common culture' ensure that wealthy Britons and their fortunes can move easily between the two. British investors have been sufficiently confident of the probity of Manx solicitors and accountants that they will nominate them directors and shareholders of companies for which the British provide the money and ideas. This is to side-step inquiries from the Inland Revenue designed to ensure that Manx-registered companies do genuinely trade from the island. Any British government which sought to introduce a wealth tax, or impose heavier taxation on the rich, would face the fact that much private as well as corporate wealth has already moved to these islands in recent years and more would certainly follow if a serious threat was perceived by the owners. It is difficult to see what a British government with an egalitarian taxation programme could do about this: the islands are self-governing, their banks and financial institutions safe from British interference. Reconquest hardly seems a possibility.

The second important development of the mid 1970s was the rise of the tax avoidance industry; several of the companies under the greatest attack (most notably, Rossminster) operated in part through companies in Guernsey and the Isle of Man.[17] Alternative methods of protecting savings in the 1960s and 1970s had proved increasingly unsatisfactory: for instance it was estimated that by April 1975 share prices were 40 per cent below the high point of mid 1972 while if inflation is taken into account the real value of equity savings had fallen to one-third of what they had been earlier. In addition capital transfer tax had to be paid.

Tax avoidance experts became increasingly self-confident. One of them, giving his name and address, wrote to *The Economist*: 'Tax avoidance is at present an important national activity because it helps to maintain the level of incentives, to assist industrial investment, to protect jobs, to pay for education, to encourage charity and so on: in fact it promotes all those things which are discouraged by the present penal rates of taxation.'[18] Tax avoidance experts were prospering and some were successful enough to become millionaires.

They became adept at detecting loopholes in the tax law and turning them to the advantage of clients. Avoidance, unlike evasion, is not illegal but what distinguishes the two very often is the ability of the person seeking to avoid tax to pay for the services of an expert advisor. The Inland Revenue was repeatedly obliged to propose legislation to close a loophole that had already been widely exploited.

The complexity and subtlety of tax avoidance schemes in the mid 1970s may be illustrated by two examples, one depending on commodity deals and the other on the introduction of new taxes themselves. The first relied on the fact that commodity markets traded for future delivery and prices were highly volatile. It was therefore possible to speculate on the price of the commodity itself, and on the difference between prices at different dates. Speculation on the latter was very much the lesser risk and it was from this element — the 'straddle' — that one scheme obtained its name. Tax avoidance companies arranged a package for individuals or companies which wished to make a loss for tax purposes. A partnership was established between this person, a commodity dealer and the tax avoidance company itself. The partnership then embarked on a series of 'straddle' transactions in a commodity which would minimise the risk of loss to fluctuations in the differential on delivery dates. The end of the accounting period was carefully chosen to show an adequate loss for tax purposes on one side of the 'straddle' and a profit on the other. Accounting practice at this time dictated that provision had to be made for the unrealised losses, but there was no compulsion to take a profit on the unrealised profits. A paper loss was thus established for the would-be tax avoider, but any profits would only become apparent in a later accounting period. The tax avoidance company then took over responsibility for sorting out the tax problems posed by the profitable side of the 'straddle'. It is clear immediately that such schemes did not in any sense represent a genuine trading operation; they took place for one reason only, to avoid tax. As such, they may have obeyed the letter of the law but they flouted its spirit and also deprived the Inland Revenue of very large sums of money. It was estimated in 1978 that over one hundred such schemes had been organised and the amounts of money involved dwarf any mentioned in the course of this study, including those in share-pushing cases. A single example, involving a large building company, showed that £2.8 million had been paid into a scheme in order to obtain a potential tax saving of over £18 million.[19]

Tax experts were also skilful at taking advantage of the possibilities of new taxes and demonstrated greater nimbleness in detecting their flaws than the civil servants and politicians who had drawn them up. There had already been several instances of this earlier in the decade when city experts produced two schemes to avoid the provisions of the capital gains tax. 'Bed and breakfast' deals enabled a company to establish a loss for tax purposes by selling shares whose price was falling in the evening and buying them back next morning: realised losses could then be used to offset gains elsewhere.

When the authorities discovered what was going on and took action against it, share speculators invented 'double-banking' whereby a firm which needed a tax loss acquired an identical amount of stock to that which it already held, and the following day sold the same amount. Capital gains tax rules stated that when selling, the first stocks bought were sold, so the investor finished with his investment intact but at a new cost price and with a tax loss as well. It may be wondered what proportion of a company's time would be spent working out and operating such schemes presumably at the expense of time spent on legitimate business matters. But the rewards in terms of tax saved presumably made it all worthwhile.

The Land Development Tax which was effective from August 1976 provided another example of the possibilities of new taxes for the tax avoider. From that date profits on property development were taxed at rates up to 80 per cent. In fact property companies had anticipated the legislation and had taken care to minimise their potential taxable profits. The basis of the avoidance schemes was in effect to buy losses on past trading which could in certain circumstances be offset against current or future profits for tax purposes. If a company possessed property assets on which it sought to avoid paying tax it bought a loss-making property company laid on by the tax expert which became a subsidiary in the main group. It then became possible to move assets around between the various subsidiary companies to place them where they could most usefully be assessed for taxation purposes.

Indications that such transactions had been taking place occurred in company reports but in a very concealed manner: usually in the form of a note referring to loss-making subsidiaries acquired and sold in the course of a year.[20] A disconcerting feature of such developments was the involvement in them of nationalised industries whose previous losses now, in the world of inflation, high taxation, and tax avoidance, actually represented assets which could be sold for tax avoidance schemes. In 1971, British Rail participated in a scheme in which its tax losses were transferred to a number of public companies (GEC, GUS) and banks (Barclay's, William and Glyn's) in exchange for inexpensive leasing finance for rolling stock and equipment. The National Coal Board was involved in a similar scheme.

Opinions differed about the best method of dealing with these developments. Two main arguments were presented about the approach that should be taken. One insisted that the tax structure must be reformed and the heavy taxation on the highly paid reduced, so that the motive for avoidance would also be reduced, if not eliminated. This was not a practical alternative for a Labour government, and critics suggested that some people would endeavour to avoid paying tax, whatever its level.

The alternative was to tighten up controls and this was the approach preferred by the government. In 1976 the Inland Revenue set up a special office in Edinburgh to tackle 'the problems' caused by 'the mushrooming oil industry'.[21] By 1981 these special offices had increased to seven, in various parts of the country, yet this was still not enough. It was anticipated that eventually fifteen would be needed to cover all the revenue regions. Each was staffed by ten to a dozen inspectors (who required 'expensive' training) backed up by a 'small' clerical staff. Furthermore the Finance Bill of 1976 proposed to give the Revenue additional powers via Section 20B of Schedule 6. These became the subject of fierce controversy. Section 20B proposed that the premises of a suspected tax fraud could be searched, by force if necessary, after a JP issued a warrant on application from an officer of the board. He was allowed to seize and remove documents and 'other things whatsoever'. These were considerable powers for peacetime and opponents argued they threatened civil liberties. 'Some Inland Revenue inspectors', *The Economist* said, 'have begun in recent years to turn into vigilantes of a most unsavoury and un-British kind.'[22]

The government eventually made concessions. The local tax inspector would need to obtain permission to search from the head office of the Inland Revenue and the warrant would have to be signed by a second-tier judge in England and Wales. There were, of course, many fewer of these than magistrates and it was thought they would not take kindly to being asked too often.

Finally the Inland Revenue announced that it was changing its methods of investigating taxpayers' accounts. Previously the board had inquired into 30 per cent of the accounts of the self-employed; from 1976-7 it would concentrate on 12 per cent, of which one-quarter would be given the 'closest' scrutiny. The board believed that greater selectivity was successful. The amount collected in tax, interest and penalties rose from £23 million in 1975-6 to £37 million in 1976-7 (though inflation was also rising fast at this time). The board also took court action more frequently to secure tax due but the number of criminal proceedings instituted was still under two hundred a year. It was also discovered at this time that arrears due under the PAYE system were mainly the result of the failure of directors to pay tax. The amount of money involved amounted to upwards of £80 million. Employees of companies had tax deducted before they were paid their wages but directors drew money without paying tax and it was apparently very difficult for the Inland Revenue to detect them. Much press reporting and political capital was made out of social security 'scrounging' yet the sum lost by comparison was small: £2.6 million a year.[23]

Towards the end of the period three important prosecutions were initiated which were thought at the time to demonstrate that the authorities were at last seriously concerned to punish companies involved in tax avoidance. All three were very expensive and occupied a considerable amount of court time. The companies were William Press Ltd; Rossminster, the tax avoidance experts; and the Vestey family trusts.

In the spring of 1979, eleven employees of the William Press group were charged with tax frauds arising from the employment of lump labour amounting to half a million pounds. In March of the previous year 150 revenue inspectors had raided eight offices of this company and taken away 'sacks' of documents. The enquiries had lasted fifteen months. Eleven persons were now charged, including the managing and finance directors. Some 3,000 documents were used to build up a case against the company and proceedings in the magistrates' courts were scrutinised by many interested parties because the prosecution was a test case. The Inland Revenue needed to carry through the prosecution convincingly because many MPs were critical of the search and seizure powers granted to the Inland Revenue in 1976 and wanted to reduce them. The number of these MPs was greatly reinforced by the Conservative election victory in May 1979.

The case finally came to trial in spring 1981 but the judge halted the proceedings after hearing the prosecution case. He criticised the 'dawn' raids as an over-reaction but also defended the Inland Revenue from accusations that they had behaved like the 'Spanish Inquisition'. He directed the jury to return verdicts of not guilty of conspiracy to defraud the Inland Revenue. Defence costs, amounting to £330,000, were to be paid from public funds. The Inland Revenue could not stand many more failures on that kind of scale.[24] The judge said that 'looking at the totality of the evidence, it would not be right to put these defendants in further jeopardy'.

It was thought that the attention of the Inland Revenue had been drawn to the Press group by a 'disgruntled' ex-employee, and this was also said to have happened with the Rossminster group. Denis Healey, while Chancellor of the Exchequer, had suggested that retrospective legislation could prove lethal for highly artificial tax-avoidance schemes like those invented by Rossminster, and would also avoid the necessity for expensive court cases.[25] Retroactive legislation against the 'straddle' was introduced, but the principle rather than the detail was more dangerous for the tax avoidance company. Such schemes were sold without guarantees but the client could be sure that they would not be caught by an existing law. Now that was no longer the position and uncertainty would inevitably hinder the marketing of schemes.

The Rossminster group had also been the victim of 'dawn raids' when seventy tax and police officials raided its Mayfair offices and a number of private homes at seven o'clock in the morning. Twelve vanloads of material were taken away, a somewhat random collection because included among them was the school report of the fourteen-year-old daughter of one of the company directors. In an action in the High Court, Lord Denning ordered the Revenue to return these materials and Rossminster agreed to store them pending an appeal. The result of the appeal, however, was to permit the Inland Revenue to sift the material which took them two years. A decision whether to prosecute had still not been taken at the end of 1981. In the interim, a decision of the House of Lords had 'virtually abolished' artificial tax avoidance. Lord Wilberforce ruled in favour of a proposal by the Inland Revenue that made tax schemes like those invented by Rossminster vulnerable in the courts.[26]

The third case, involving the Vestey family trusts, produced an answer as little satisfactory to the authorities as that concerning the Press group. In 1970 the tax authorities began to enquire into capital distributions amounting to over £2.5 million made to six members of the Vestey family between 1962 and 1966. The result was that these beneficiaries were assessed for an extra £5 million in income tax and surtax. Court proceedings over the matter began at once and a lower court reduced the assessment 'somewhat'. The Law Lords, however, decided that the relevant section of the 1952 income tax act was not intended to hold 'endless' generations liable for the fiscal sins of their fathers. The Vestey family was in effect entitled to the tax-free enjoyment of the £2.5 million, a decision which narrowed the Inland Revenue's discretionary scope in pursuing tax avoiders. The new Chancellor of the Exchequer, Sir Geoffrey Howe, duly announced that he was going to close this legal loophole, a measure that was rendered the more necessary by the abolition of exchange controls. This made transferring currency to offshore tax havens easier. It was suggested by the Revenue that tax avoided in schemes of the Vestey type may already have approached as much as £1 billion a year.[27]

In May 1979 the Conservative Party won the general election. It now became possible for an experiment to be made in the 'alternative theory' about the relationship between high taxation and tax avoidance. According to *The Economist*, Mrs Thatcher had 'shouted her first priority . . . from every husting in the country: reduce taxation.' Marginal rates in particular were so high that 'avoidance is regarded by many as not only morally justified but even as economically necessary if the right people are to be given the incentives they need, not only in their own interests but in the interests of the economy as a whole.'[28] Accordingly the top rate of tax on income was reduced from 90 per cent to 60 per cent in one of the first financial acts of the new government. It has proved much more difficult to be similarly generous to the rest of the population. Whether the measure has had a significant impact on the extent of tax avoidance has yet to be seen.

Notes

Introduction
(pp. 1-18)
1. *The Guardian*, 3 March 1983.
2. Ibid.
3. Ibid., 18 March 1983.
4. *The Times*, 11 March 1981.
5. *The Times*, 4 July 1983.
6. *Sunday Mirror*, 30 January 1977.
7. *The Sun*, 9 August 1976.
8. *Financial Times*, 12 May 1981.
9. A. Dilnot and C. N. Morris, 'What do we know about the Black Economy?' in *Fiscal Studies*, March 1981.
10. *The Guardian*, 7 May 1981.
11. *The Guardian*, 20 July 1981.
12. *Lloyds Bank Review*, July 1981, pp. 58-9.
13. The Outer Circle Policy Unit, *Policing the Hidden Economy: the Significance of Control and Fiddles* (1978), p. 5.
14. There, bread salesmen had an 'average' theft income which 'sometimes' amounted to 10 per cent of their GSV (gross sales volume). Four per cent of GSV was fiddled from customers. In case this figure was exaggerated the Unit halved it and projected it to the 'visible' part of the service industries (those in which workers had face-to-face dealings with the public and exchanged goods for money). The contribution of the service industries to GNP was £35, 240m (48 per cent of GNP). The fiddled income at 2 per cent was £705m a year. (pp. 11-12).
15. *Lloyds Bank Review*, p. 59.
16. V. Gatrell, *Crime and the Law* (1980), p. 240.
17. D. Philips, *Crime and Authority in Victorian England* (1977), pp. 23-4.
18. J. P. Martin, *Offenders as Employees* (1962), p. 86.
19. For the definition of 'serious' used in this study see below p. 22.
20. Approximately the LCC boroughs of Hackney, Shoreditch, Stoke Newington, Bethnal Green and parts of Stepney. Offences committed in these districts were sent for hearing to these courts.
21. Certain newspapers have been used to trace proceedings and will

be indicated in references by their initials: *The Barnsley Chronicle* (BC), *The Birkenhead News and Wirral General Advertiser* (BN), *The Brighton Gazette* (BG), *The Brighton and Hove Gazette* (BHG), *The Hackney and Kingsland Gazette* (HG), and *The Walsall Observer* (WO).

22. C. A. Moser and Wolf Scott, *British Towns: a statistical study of their social and economic differences* (1961), Appendix B.
23. Birkenhead £12 12s 0d, Walsall £11 16s 0d, Barnsley £10 10s 0d.
24. *Birkenhead and Its Manufactures. Official Handbook* (1920).
25. *Official Handbook* (1933 edn.), p. 17.
26. *Walsall and Its Industrial Advantages* (1917), pp. 5-7.
27. *Handbook*, 1933, p. 17.
28. Louis Heren, *Growing Up Poor in London* (1973), p. 108.
29. Sydney Horler, *London's Underworld* (1934), p. 210.
30. John Pearson, *The Profession of Violence* (1973), p. 28.
31. Sir Cyril Burt, *The Young Delinquent* (1925), p. 37.
32. F. Sharpe, *Sharpe of the Flying Squad* (1938), p. 171.
33. Peter Willmott, *Adolescent Boys of East London* (Rev. Edn. 1969), pp. 145-147.
34. R. Lawton and C. M. Cunningham, *Merseyside. Social and Economic Studies* (1970), p. 39.
35. Birkenhead, *Police Report*, 1921.
36. Public Assistance Committee.
37. Ibid., 1930.
38. BN, September 1932.
39. Patrick Hamilton, *Hangover Square* (1941), p. 133; Heren, *op. cit.*, p. 74.
40. County Borough of Brighton, *The Chief Constable's Report on the Police Establishment with Criminal and other Statistics*, 1930-1951. Police reports for Walsall are 'inaccessible' while those for Barnsley have apparently been mislaid.

Chapter 2
(pp. 19-37)
1. Sir William Beveridge, *British Food Control* (1928), p. 146.
2. *East End News*, 29 January 1918.
3. BG, 9 January 1918.
4. HG, 9 February 1917.
5. HG, 28 March 1917.
6. Beveridge, *Food Control*, p. 204.
7. *Dictionary of National Biography*, 1931-1940.
8. *Food Control*, pp. 34-5.
9. Ibid., p. 185.
10. HG, 28 March 1917.
11. HG, 30 May 1917.
12. Beveridge, *Food Control*, p. 217.
13. Beveridge, *Food Control*, p. 231.

14. A minimum fine of £50 has been chosen to distinguish serious from minor black market offences. It appears from the comments they made in court that some magistrates placed the differentiating point much lower down the financial scale, sometimes as low as £10. But a fine of £50 or more admits of no dispute: here magistrates believed they were punishing a serious offence.
15. HG, 27 August 1917.
16. HG, 28 December 1917.
17. cf. HG, 9 January 1918.
18. HG, 21 July 1919.
19. HG, 11 August 1919.
20. WO, 22 December 1917.
21. A decision of King's Bench required that there should be a separate summons in respect of each article of food, instead of the entire hoard being included in a single summons.
22. *National Food Journal*, 10 April 1918.
23. Fined £50 or more or imprisoned.
24. The Ritz and the Carlton were both heavily fined.
25. BG, 9 January 1918.
26. BG, 19 January 1918.
27. BG, 2 February 1918.
28. BG, 2 March 1918.
29. BG, 15 June 1918.
30. *East End News*, 16 March 1917.
31. Ibid, 20 April 1917; 26 June 1917.
32. *East End News*, 7 September 1917.
33. *The National Food Journal*, 1917-18.
34. Beveridge, *Food Control*, p. 205.
35. *National Food Journal*, 12 December 1917.
36. *East End News*, 10 May 1918.
37. Ibid., 25 January 1918.
38. The Procurator Fiscal in Glasgow alleged that 'Jewish bakers in the city had set up a system of spies, who watched the food inspectors and made it difficult to get evidence.' *National Food Journal*, 10 April 1918.
39. Ibid., 24 July 1918.
40. One bought nearly 10,000 lbs of meat in a single month.
41. Gerd Hardach, *The First World War 1914-1918* (1978), pp. 119, 200.

    Food prices in Great Britain

	1914	1917	1919
bread per 4 lbs	5¾d	11½d	9d
beef per 1 lb	7¾d	1s 4¾d	1s 3¾d
butter per 1lb	1s 2½d	1s 11¾d	2s 6d
milk per quart	3½d	5½d	7¼d
sugar per 1 lb	2d	6d	7d

    Beveridge, *Food Control*, p. 371.
42. *The National Food Journal*, 13 March 1918.

43. BG, 13 October 1917.
44. BG, 12 December 1917.
45. *East End News*, 25 January 1918.
46. Ibid., 26 January 1917.
47. *The National Food Journal*, 20 March 1920.
48. Father was a Wesleyan who had signed the pledge but when the shop closed at the end of the day he would often go down to the pub for a drink. Lillian Beckwith, *About my Father's Business* (1971), p. 73.
49. HG, 8 October 1913.
50. HG, 15 October 1913.
51. HG, 27 August 1917.
52. *Report of the Commissioner of Police of the Metropolis for the Years 1918 and 1919*, Cmd. 543.
53.

	Birkenhead	Barnsley	Brighton	Walsall
1913	16	7	7	16
1917	32	0	18	8

54. BC, 4 January 1913; WO, 1 February 1913.
55. BN, 2 August 1913.
56. BN, 26 May 1917.
57. BC, 4 January 1913; WO, 1 February 1913.
58. BG, 28 March 1917.
59. Number convicted of stealing

	Food	Alcohol	Cloth	Metals
1913	11	0	13	20
1917	39	7	17	9

60. HG, 4 August 1913.
61. HG, 7 November 1917.
62. HG, 27 July 1917; 15 August 1917.
63. HG, 30 April 1913.
64. BN, 7 March 1917.
65. BG, 21 February 1917; 17 March 1917.
66. BN, 2 August 1913.
67. BN, 2 May 1917.
68. HG, 27 August 1917; 7 November 1917.
69. *The National Food Journal*, 14 August 1918.
70. Beveridge, *Food Control*, p. 237.
71. Hardach, p. 120, 200.

Chapter 3
(pp. 38-63)
1. *National Food Journal*, 10 March 1920.
2. *Birkenhead Advertiser*, 25 December 1918.
3. *National Food Journal*, 15 October 1919.
4. Ibid., 28 November 1917.
5. *National Food Journal*, 12 March 1919, 26 March 1919.

6. Cases reported in *The National Food Journal*

	number	% involving meat & poultry	alcohol
Dec. 25 1918 - Mar. 26 1919	71	48	6
Apr. 9 1919 - Jul. 9 1919	70	60	16
Aug. 13 1919 - Nov. 12 1919	90	51	22

7. Hendon and District Archeological Society, *Those Were the Days* (1980), p. 16.
8. HG, 17 January 1919.
9. HG, 14 February 1919.
10. HG, 30 June 1919.
11. Cf. the fate of George Johnson, a loader on the Great Western. He took three pints worth 1s 6d, watered the rest to make up the difference, was prosecuted and jailed for twenty-one days. HG, 17 December 1919.
12. A. J. P. Taylor, *English History 1914-45* (1970 edn.), p. 66.
13. HG, 11 August 1919.
14. *Food Control*, p. 289.
15. HG, 7 January 1920.
16. HG, 8 October 1919.
17. HG, 10 October 1919.
18. *National Food Journal*, 15 October 1919.
19. HG, 17 December 1919.
20. HG, 6 June 1921.
21. Mowat, p. 125.
22. HG, 6 June 1921.
23. HG, 15 April 1921.
24. Average fines

	1919	1918
England	£4 14s 3d	£4 8s 4d
Scotland	£3 12s 1d	£3 5s 3d
Wales	£4 2s 4d	£4 16s 4d

25. *East End News*, 26 April 1921.

27. BN, 7 June 1919.
28. HG, 22 December 1919.
29. She had had a university education and was said in court to be 'a woman of superior education, of considerable travel, and a fluent linguist.' BG, 18 March 1922.
30. *Report of the Commissioner of Police of the Metropolis*, 1920, Cmd. 1294; 1921, Cmd. 1699; 1922, Cmd. 1904.
31. Phillip Knightley, *The Vestey Affair* (1981).
32. Ibid., p. 28.
33. Knightley, p. 36.
34. HG, 15 January 1932; 27 July 1932.
35. HG, 20 May 1932.
36. HG, 20 June 1934.
37. In north London there were eight convictions of clothing manufac-

turers in 1932 and ten in 1937, five of furniture manufacturers in 1932 and three in 1937, four of builders in 1932 and three in 1937, and four of shopkeepers in 1932 (one in 1937).

38. HG, 26 February 1937.
39. *Birkenhead and Cheshire Advertiser*, 2 July 1932.
40. WO, 13 August 1932.
41. HG, 3 September 1928.
42. HG, 1 April 1932; 22 July 1932.
43. Jackson, *Crime*, p. 72.
44. *News of the World*, 10 April 1927, 20 July 1930; HG, 15 January 1934.
45. Cf. *News of the World*, 25 October 1931.
46. Dorothy Scannell, *Dolly's Mixture* (1977), pp. 90-93.
47. *News of the World*, 23 September 1934; 15 October 1934; 30 June 1935.
48. Ibid., 25 November 1934.
49. Ibid., 30 June 1935.
50. *News of the World*, 10 February 1935.
51. Ibid., 14 May 1939; 15 May 1932.
52. Ibid., 2 October 1932.
53. *News of the World*, 11 September 1938.
54. Ibid., 21 March 1937; 5 February 1933.
55. *Sharepushing. Report of the Departmental Committee Appointed by the Board of Trade 1936-37* (Cmd. 5539).
56. *West London Press*, 28 January 1938.
57. *News of the World*, 22 January 1928.
58. Ibid., 26 October 1930.
59. Ibid., 30 October 1927.
60. Ibid., 22 January 1928.
61. *News of the World*, 2 June 1935.
62. The report commented – presumably referring to evidence it had heard – 'prompt police action . . . is essential and it is certainly not in the public interest to inform a complainant who has already lost his money that the police would render every assistance after he has assumed the role of prosecutor . . . on his own responsibility' (p. 29).
63. City of London Police, *Report, Police Committee, submitting Report of Commissioners for the Year*, 1931-1940.
64. Senior ranks in the force suffered a total pay cut of 10 per cent.
65. *Sharepushing*, p. 28.
66. *News of the World*, 26 September 1937.
67. Jim Phelan, *The Underworld* (1953), p. 35. Cf. the remark by Edwin Sutherland's professional thief: 'It is impossible to beat an honest man in a confidence game.' *The Professional Thief* (1937), p. 69.
67. HG, 5 February 1932; 7 March 1932; 26 October 1932; 20 June 1932.
68. HG, 1 September 1937.

69. BC, 11 September 1937.

70. WO, 9 April 1932; 16 April 1932.

71. Nancy Sharman, *Nothing to Steal: the Story of a Southampton Childhood* (1977), p. 34.

72. A. S. Jasper, *A Hoxton Childhood* (1969).

73. Ron Barnes, *Coronation Cups and Jam Jars* (1976), p. 56.

74. In the early 1970s accounting systems took note of pilfering losses in the form of 'stock shrinkage', for which a figure of between two per cent and 5 per cent was considered acceptable. Henry, p. 30.

75. HG, 16 February 1934.

76. HG, 20 June 1928.

77. HG, 18 January 1932.

78. He said (*a*) he bought them at a post office, (*b*) he bought them from a man he met at a football match, (*c*) he bought them from a man he met in a billiard hall. HG, 24 December 1928.

79. HG, 30 November 1932.

80. Including Herbert Finn who 'had given a great deal of trouble since 1921' and Samuel Cohen ('since 1923 the department had expended a considerable amount of time and money in dealing with him') HG, 15 January 1932.

Chapter 4
(pp. 64-84)

1. Joe Jacobs, *Out of the Ghetto* (1978), p. 35.

2. Cf. Albert Speer, *Inside the Third Reich* (1970), p. 256.

3. Cases in which fines of £50 or more or imprisonment were imposed.

4. HG, 8 January 1941.

5. HG, 20 October 1941.

6. HG, 6 February 1942.

7. HG, 5 October 1942. The magistrate fined him and his wife £65.

8. HG, 21 April 1943.

9. HG, 24 July 1944; 22 September 1944.

10. BN, 12 April 1944.

11. BN, 8 September 1943.

12. WO, 2 January 1943.

13. The goods they bought were given to the Civic Guild of Help. WO, 16 January 1944.

14. WO, 19 June 1943; 17 July 1943; 14 August 1943.

15. BHG, 27 February 1943.

16. BHG, 15 July 1944.

17. WO, 13 November 1943.

18. BHG, 19 May 1945.

19. BHG, 12 February 1944.

20. BHG, 26 August 1944.

21. *Willesden Chronicle*, 10 January 1944.

22. HG, 15 September 1943.

23. *Willesden Chronicle*, 10 March 1944; 26 May 1944.

24. HG, 20 September 1943.

25. HG, 17 March 1944.
26. HG, 6 October 1943.
27. HG, 16 October 1944; 10 November 1944.
28. WO, 17 July 1943.
29. City of Leeds, *Chief Constable's Annual Reports*, 1938-1946.
30. Cf. Edward Smithies, *Crime in Wartime* (1982), Chapter three.
31. *Report of the Commissioner of Police of the Metropolis for the Year 1944* (Cmd. 6627).
32. *The Star*, 22 September 1944.
33. Charles Raven, *Underworld Nights* (1956), p. 128.
34. Number of convictions of persons aged 18 and over:

	Barnsley	Birkenhead	Brighton	N. London	Walsall
1937	6	1	3	47	0
1941	4	70	2	135	4
1944	5	42	5	133	1

35. *Barnsley Chronicle*, 26 October 1941.
36. BC, 27 December 1941.
37. WO, 19 April 1941.
38. BHG, 22 April 1944.
39. BN, 15 January 1941.
40. BN, 20 August 1941.
41. BN, 23 April 1941.
42. Undated letter (Dec? 1941) from T. Garnett of NDLC. PRO Bk 1/38.
43. Chief Constable's reports, 1941-4.
44. BN, 10 May 1944.
45. Similar claims were made by a furnisher's, losing £2,000 worth of goods a month (1942); a flour factor's: £500 per quarter (1942); Western's Laundries paid £200 a week in insurance claims (1944); Charrington's Brewery lost 354 dozen bottles in six months (1944); US Army Stores 7,610 ladies silk stockings in five months (1944); 600 stands of timber went in 12 months (1944), etc.
46. HG, 3 January 1941.
47. HG, 21 July 1941.
48. HG, 20 October 1944. The owner's value of the carton was £25. The magistrate fined Morris £10.
49. 250 cigarettes worth 29s (one month), tin of paint worth £2 (one month), meat worth 15s (one month), beef worth 10s (two months). All these men had 'good' characters; all lost their jobs.
50. HG, 4 July 1941; 8 August 1941.
51. HG, 18 July 1941.
52. HG, 8 December 1941.
53. HG, 21 July 1941.
54. HG, 3 December 1941.
55. HG, 2 August 1944.
56. Marshall B. Clinard, *The Black Market* (1952), p. 27.
57. Carlo M. Cipolla (ed), *The Fontana Economic History of Europe. Contemporary Economies. Part One* (1976), p. 23, 40.

58. François Caron, *An Economic History of Modern France* (1979), pp. 270-1.
59. Cipolla, *op. cit*, p. 211.

Chapter 5
(pp. 85-110)
1. WO, 3 July 1948.
2. WO, 14 August 1948.
3. BN, 7 August 1948.
4. George Orwell, *1984* (Penguin edn.), pp. 59-60.
5. Number of convictions for serious offences

	1945	1946	1947	1948	1949	1950
Barnsley	2	1	4	3	0	1
Birkenhead	2	1	2	12	7	8
Brighton	1	3	6	11	6	9
Walsall	2	0	0	2	3	3

6. HG, 15 April 1946.
7. HG, 5 September 1945.
8. HG, 26 November 1945.
9. HG, 21 June 1946.
10. *East London Advertiser*, 30 August 1946; 25 July 1947.
11. *East London Advertiser*, 25 July 1947.
12. BN, 9 February 1946; 13 July 1946.
13. *East London Advertiser*, 29 August 1947.
14. The exception made £7,000 worth of furniture without a licence. His illegal profits amounted to £750. HG, 29 August 1947.
15. Sentencing, the magistrate Daniel Hopkin, said, 'There is nothing worse for the country than this black market business. You see its effects in other countries like France and Italy. It is literally killing those countries, and it is in order to stop this country sharing in that situation that no leniency can be shown in these cases.' HG, 28 May 1947.
16. *East London Advertiser*, 9 May 1947.
17. *East London Advertiser*, 16 May 1947.
18. HG, 16 June 1947; 20 October 1947; 17 December 1947.
19. BN, 25 August 1945.
20. BN, 18 February 1948.
21. BC, 10 January 1948; 16 February 1948; 1 December 1948.
22. HG, 18 October 1946.
23. *East London Advertiser*, 25 April 1947.
24. Ibid., 28 March 1947.
25. Ibid., 21 March 1947.
26. Neville Faulks, *No Mitigating Circumstances* (1977), pp. 146-7.
27. BC, 13 December 1947.
28. BC, 8 March 1947; 31 May 1947.
29. Only part of the Ministry of Food files for Brighton in the Public Record Office are open to the public.

30. BHG, 31 May 1947.
31. BHG, 21 June 1947.
32. BHG, 24 January 1948.
33. BHG, 17 April 1948; 31 July 1948.
34. BHG, 2 October 1948.
35. Stanley Wade Baron, *The Contact Man: the Story of Sidney Stanley and the Lynskey Tribunal* (1966).
36. *The Times*, 2 May 1974.
37. M. Gillard and M. Tomkinson, *Nothing to Declare: the Political Corruption of John Poulson* (1981); R. Fitzwalter and D. Taylor, *Web of Corruption* (1981).
38. John Williams, *Hume: Portrait of a Double Murderer* (1960); Ivan Butler, *Trials of Brian Donald Hume* (1976); Rebecca West, *A Train of Powder* (1955).
39. BC, 25 February 1950.
40. WO, 8 January 1949; 30 April 1949.
41. BHG, 24 September 1949.
42. HG, 27 January 1950.
43. The exception was the smuggling by three men of several thousand Swiss watches. HG, 30 November 1949.
44. HG, 14 October 1949.
45. He fined them £5,000. HG, 11 March 1949.
46. HG, 23 January 1950; 12 July 1950.
47. Hill, p. 140.
48. S. Pollard, *The Development of the British Economy 1914-1967* (1969 edn), p. 344, 397.
49. P. Calvocoressi, *The British Experience 1945-75* (1978), p. 110.
50. BHG, 22 July 1944.
51. BHG, 5 August 1944.
52. Through the medium of the *Hackney Gazette*, *South London Press* and *Kensington Post*, all of which gave generous coverage to the proceedings of local courts.
53. HG, 22 March 1946.
54. He was fined £4,500. *South London Press*, 17 April 1942; 24 April 1942.
55. HG, 10 March 1947; 14 May 1947.
56. HG, 1 October 1941. The 1944 case concerned less than £3 worth of arrears.
57. *East London Advertiser*, 24 February 1950.
58. The figure for Brighton in 1950 is not reliable: the *Brighton and Hove Gazette* ceased to report all court cases involving this type of offence.
59. BN, 8 February 1947.
60. *Report*, 1947.
61. BN, 1 March 1947.
62. HG, 24 February 1947.
63. The matches were worth £3 0s 3d. HG, 14 May 1947.
64. *East London Advertiser*, 21 March 1947; 23 May 1947.

65. HG, 19 December 1947.
66. HG, 31 December 1947.
67. HG, 8 December 1950.
68. HG, 20 December 1950.
69. HG, 27 November 1950. In 1947 Rowland Thomas heard a case in which a young knife grinder admitted taking £16 worth of tobacco and selling it. He pleaded his wages were too low (they were £5 10s a week). Thomas expressed sympathy and fined him.
70. *The Times*, 8 April 1948.
71. *The Times*, 4 May 1948.
72. Brighton bench fined people found with forged coupons while a Londoner with enough to buy 400 gallons was fined £250. BHG, 9 October 1948; HG, 12 September 1949.
73. *The Times*, 19 October 1948.

Chapter 6
(pp. 111-128)
1. Sked and Cook, *Post-War Britain*, p. 11.
2. For a discussion of the 'stop-go' cycle, see S. Pollard, *The Development of the British Economy, 1914-1967* (1969), pp. 468-84.
3. *East London Advertiser*, 28 October 1949.
4. A strike in 1959 from 22 June to 4 August closed all the local newspapers in these towns except for the *Walsall Observer* which managed to publish a limited edition.
5. BC, 23 June 1956; 13 February 1965.
6. WO, 1 November 1968.
7. Birkenhead, *Police Report*, 1955, 1962.
8. Ibid., 1965, 1966.
9. Birkenhead, *Police Report*, 1966.
10. BN, 23 December 1953.
11. BN, 7 April 1956; 2 August 1968.
12. HG, 20 March 1959.
13. He told the magistrate he had been ill, off work and receiving no pay, but he had nine children to support. He made a good impression: the magistrate decided 'the country would not benefit' if he went to jail and conditionally discharged him. His employer 'thought so highly' of him that he gave him his job back. Less fortunate was a railway porter who sold bottles of whisky to a pub manager. Eighteen bottles were mentioned in charges; the two men were jailed for six months apiece. HG, 29 May 1959; 8 September 1959.
14. HG, 26 September 1956.
15. HG, 6 February 1953.
16. Pollard, p. 425.
17. HG, 6 April 1965.
18. In 1962 people were prosecuted for taking dog biscuits worth £2 5s 0d ('to feed his dog'), deodorant worth £1 4s 0d ('a present

for his girl friend'), underclothes (valued at 5s 8d), 15s worth of lead, two bottles of sauce, two nightgowns (shop price £2), and £4 worth of paint. In 1968 people were taken to court for stealing food worth 16s 2d, bacon worth 2s 6d, tea worth 3s 6d, lead valued at £3, £8 worth of rope, paint brushes (£2), a towel with a shop price of 5s 11d, and two cardigans which would have sold for £2 11s 0d.

19. HG, 16 February 1953.
20. HG, 25 July 1956.
21. HG, 19 June 1962. Two other men were retained that year but in 1965 there were none. In 1968 four people were kept on, two of them 18 year olds employed by Hackney council.
22. A dock labourer stole £28 worth of whisky, admitted eight other thefts during the previous twelve months, had two earlier convictions for theft and was jailed for six months. Two other men jailed also had records (as did several who were fined) while the fourth was a security officer. He had stolen clothing worth £2 15 0d but was jailed because he was 'supposed to prevent thefts'. BN, 23 June 1956.
23. One sold two stolen bottles of gin for a pound, told the court 'he had been drinking heavily since his family was killed in the last war' and was jailed for three months; the other took 400 cigarettes and was jailed for six months. BN, 11 August 1962.
24. HG, 18 June 1965.
25. HG, 6 July 1965.
26. In the cases I have been able to trace.
27. HG, 13 April 1965; 15 April 1965; 21 May 1965.
28. BN, 5 April 1941.
29. HG, 12 October 1953.
30. HG, 9 November 1953.
31. HG, 13 November 1953.
32. HG, 26 November 1968. E. C. S. Russell, magistrate at Old Street, made similar criticisms. HG, 6 December 1968.
33. HG, 26 November 1968.
34. BC, 23 March 1968.
35. HG, 10 August 1962; WO, 31 August 1956.
36. HG, 8 May 1950.
37. HG, 17 August 1965.
38. Madeleine Kerr, *The People of Ship Street* (1958), p. 125.
39. WO, 31 May 1968.
40. BN, 13 June 1953.
41. BN, 17 March 1956.
42. BN, 15 June 1965.
43. In 1967 Birkenhead police department was merged with the Cheshire police force.
44. HG, 27 July 1953.
45. HG, 12 March 1956; 1 April 1959; 7 August 1959.

Chapter 7
(pp. 129-146)
1. Martin, pp. 17, 86.
2. A representative of the company told the court the men would not be dismissed. The magistrate put them on probation. HG, 22 July 1946.
3. *The Guardian*, 11 March 1983.
4. Martin, pp. 104, 106, 128.
5. *The Economist*, 18 April 1970.
6. Sked and Cook, *Post-War Britain*, p. 291.
7. *Economist*, 4 November 1972.
8. *Economist*, 23 June 1973; 19 April 1975; 9 June 1979.
9. Sked and Cook, p. 341.
10. *Economist*, 18 May 1973; 12 October 1974.
11. This proposal was later dropped.
12. S. Henry, *The Hidden Economy* (1978), p. 144.
13. *The Times*, 11 February 1982.
14. *Financial Times*, 9 July 1981; *Economist*, 24 May 1975.
15. *Financial Times*, 9 July 1981; p. 11.
16. The names of the Isle of Man, Jersey and Guernsey constantly recur in newspaper reports about tax avoidance. Cf. especially *Private Eye*, 23 October 1981; 10 September 1982; 20 May, 1983.
17. Cf. *Private Eye*, 3 July 1981.
18. *The Economist*, 8 May 1976.
19. *Economist*, 7 January 1978.
20. *Economist*, 7 January 1978.
21. *Financial Times*, 8 August 1981.
22. *Economist*, 1 March 1975.
23. *New Society*, 23 February 1978.
24. *Gvardian*, 3 July 1981; 4 July 1981.
25. *Economist*, 15 April 1978.
26. *Private Eye*, 3 July 1981; *Economist* 21 March, 1981.
27. *Economist*, 11 October 1980; 22 August 1981.
28. Ibid., 5 May 1979; 18 April 1970.

Bibliography

Newspapers and Journals
The Barnsley Chronicle
Birkenhead and Cheshire Advertiser
The Birkenhead News and Wirral General Advertiser
Boroughs of Poplar and Stepney and East London Advertiser
The Brighton Gazette
The Brighton and Hove Gazette
East End News
The Economist
The Hackney and Kingsland Gazette
The National Food Journal
The News of the World
New Society
Private Eye
South London Press
The Walsall Observer

Police Reports
City of Leeds, *Chief Constable's Annual Reports*, 1938-46
City of London Police, *Report, Police Committee*, 1931-8
County Borough of Brighton, *The Chief Constable's Report on the Police Establishment with Criminal and other Statistics*, 1928-61
Watch Committee of the Borough of Birkenhead, *The Chief Constable's Report on the Police Establishment including Criminal Statistics*, 1928-66

Secondary and other works
Aldcroft, D. H., *The Inter-War Economy, 1919-1939* (1970)
Barnes, R., *Coronation Cups and Jam Jars* (1976)
Baron, S. W., *The Contact Man: The Story of Sidney Stanley and the Lynskey Tribunal* (1966)
Beckwith, L., *About My Father's Business* (1971)
Bermant, C., *Point of Arrival* (1975)
Beveridge, W., *British Food Control* (1928)
Breed, B., *White Collar Bird* (1979)
Butler, I., *Trials of Brian Donald Hume* (1976)

Calvocoressi, P., *The British Experience 1945-75* (1978)

Caron, F., *An Economic History of Modern France* (1979)

Cipolla, C. M., ed., *The Fontana Economic History of Europe: Contemporary Economies, Part One* (1976)

Clinard, M. B., *The Black Market* (1952)

Cressey, D. R., *Theft of the Nation* (1969)

Cronin, J.E. and Jonathan Schneer, *Social Conflict and the Political Order in Modern Britain* (1982)

Dash, J., *Good Morning, Brother* (1969)

Ditton, J., *Part-Time Crime* (1977)

Ditton, J., *Contrololology: Beyond the New Criminology* (1979)

Faulks, N., *No Mitigating Circumstances* (1977)

Faulks, N., *A Law Unto Myself* (1978)

Fitzwalter, R. and D. Taylor, *Web of Corruption* (1981)

Gatrell, V., *Crime and the Law* (1980)

Hall, S. et al., *Policing the Crisis* (1978)

Hardach, G., *The First World War 1914-1918* (1973)

Harris, J., *William Beveridge: a Biography* (1977)

Henry, S., *The Hidden Economy* (1978)

Heren, L., *Growing up Poor in London* (1973)

Hill, B., *Boss of Britain's Underworld* (1955)

Horler, S., *London's Underworld* (1934)

Jackson, Sir R., *Occupied with Crime* (1967)

Jackson, M., *Labour Relations on the Docks* (1973)

Jacobs, J., *Out of the Ghetto* (1978)

Jasper, A. S., *A Hoxton Childhood* (1969)

Kerr, M., *The People of Ship Street* (1958)

Klockars, C. B., *The Professional Fence* (1974)

Knightley, P., *The Vestey Affair* (1981)

Lawton, R. and C. M. Cunningham, eds., *Merseyside. Social and Economic Studies* (1970)

Mack, J. A., *The Crime Industry* (1975)

Mannheim, H., *Social Aspects of Crime in England between the Wars* (1940)

Mannheim, H., *Criminal Justice and Social Reconstruction* (1946)

Marwick, A., *The Deluge* (1965)

Mays, J. B., *Growing up in the City* (1954)

Martin, J. P., *Offenders as Employees* (1962)

McClintock, F. H. and N. H. Avison, *Crime in England and Wales* (1968)

Milward, A. S., *The German Economy at War* (1965)

Milward, A. S., *The Economic Effects of the World Wars on Britain* (1970)

Moser, C. A. and Wolf Scott, *British Towns* (1961)

Mowat, C. L., *Britain between the Wars 1918-1940* (1955)

Niall, I., *The Village Policeman* (1971)

Outer Circle Policy Unit, *Policing the Hidden Economy: the Significance of Control and Fiddles* (1978)

Philips, D., *Crime and Authority in Victorian England* (1977)

Pollard, S., *The Development of the British Economy, 2nd Edn 1914-1967* (1969)

Raven, C., *Underworld Nights* (1956)

Scannell, D., *Dolly's Mixture* (1977)

Sharman, N., *Nothing to Steal: the Story of a Southampton Childhood* (1977)

Sharpe, F. D., *Sharpe of the Flying Squad* (1938)

Sissons, M. and P. French, *The Age of Austerity, 1945-1951* (1964)

Sked, A. and C. Cook, *Post-War Britain. A Political History* (1979)

Smithies, E., *Crime in Wartime* (1982)

Sutherland, E. H., *The Professional Thief* (1937)

Sutherland, E. H., *White Collar Crime* (1949)

Walker, N., *Crimes, Courts and Figures* (1971)

Waller, P. J., *Democracy and Sectarianism* (1981)

Walsh, D. P., *Shoplifting. Controlling a Major Crime* (1978)

Warner, M., ed., *The Sociology of the Workplace* (1973)

West, R., *A Train of Powder* (1955)

Wilson, D.F., *Dockers: the Impact of Industrial Change* (1972)

Williams, J., *Hume — Portrait of a Double Murderer* (1960)

Willmott, P., *Adolescent Boys of East London* (1966)

Young, M. and P. Willmott, *Family and Kinship in East London* (1957)

Lord Woolton, *The Memoirs of the Rt Hon. The Earl of Woolton* (1959)

Index